Collins

Peak D

Park Rangers
Favourite Walks

National Parks | PEAK DISTRICT NATIONAL PARK

Published by Collins
An imprint of HarperCollins*Publishers*
Westerhill Road, Bishopbriggs, Glasgow G64 2QT
collins.reference@harpercollins.co.uk
www.harpercollins.co.uk

HarperCollins*Publishers*
1st Floor, Watermarque Building, Ringsend Road, Dublin 4, Ireland

Printed in Bosnia and Herzegovina

ISBN   978-0-00-843912-5   10 9 8 7 6 5 4 3 2 1

MIX
Paper from
responsible sources
FSC™ C007454

Contents

WALK LOCATIONS

▼ Recommended starting point for each route – refer to individual walk instructions for more details.

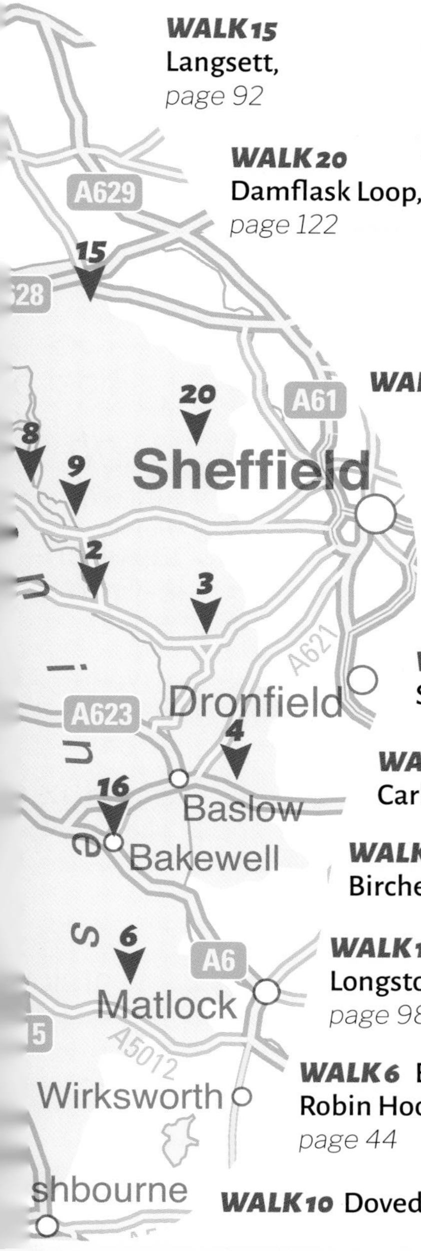
A629
15
28
20
A61
8
9
Sheffield
2
3
A621
Dronfield
A623
4
16
Baslow
Bakewell
6
A6
Matlock
5
A5012
Wirksworth
shbourne

WALK 15 Langsett, *page 92*

WALK 20 Damflask Loop, *page 122*

WALK 8 Pike Low, *page 52*

WALK 9 The Thornhill Trot, *page 60*

WALK 19 Mam Tor via the Great Ridge, *page 114*

WALK 2 Shatton Moor, *page 24*

WALK 3 Carl Wark and Higger Tor, *page 30*

WALK 4 Birchen Edge, *page 34*

WALK 16 Longstone Ashford Loop, *page 98*

WALK 6 Elton and Robin Hood's Stride, *page 44*

WALK 10 Dovedale, *page 66*

Sheep grazing on
Parkhouse Hill
at sunrise

Introduction

Set in the heart of England, the 555 square miles (1,437 sq km) of the Peak District deliver a perfect first taste of the National Park experience for everyone: from the brooding Dark Peak uplands, to the snaking valleys, rivers and drystone wall-encased fields of the southern White Peak.

The UK's first ever National Park, today this landscape that is home to nearly 40,000 people offers a bustling and adventurous location for all to enjoy – from those seeking a new or first-time outdoor experience to the seasoned enthusiast. Whether your favourite day out is clinging to a rockface, sampling the best in local food or blowing away the stresses of life on two wheels (or four legs), there's something for you in the Peak District.

Travelling into the area from the great northern cities of Sheffield, Leeds or Manchester, you'll be greeted by rolling moorlands that burst into a riot of purple in late summer every year and where shimmering reservoirs hold more history than meets the eye. Via Nottingham or Derby to the south a very different picture awaits: secretive valleys of quiet tranquillity; villages with regional fayre that's sure to tempt you; and rivers that echo to wildlife that find a home in the tumbling waters.

Whatever your age or ability, there's often no better way to immerse yourself into the Peak District than on over 35 miles (56 km) of traffic-free, multi-user trails. These former rail lines provide level, easily accessible ways to discover the history of the area with plenty of places to take a break or grab a bite to eat.

The iconic Pennine Way running up the spine of England has its start in the Peak District. This 256-mile (412 km) route, founded in 1965, is a firm favourite with thousands of visitors each year – whether taking it at a leisurely pace or as part of record-breaking time trials. The fact that the route traditionally begins in an Edale pub in the picturesque Hope Valley is perhaps an added incentive for some.

With 1,600 miles (2,575 km) of public rights of way including 64 miles (103 km) accessible to those with limited mobility, there's sure to be a quiet corner or view that makes a lasting impression.

If it's your wild side that you're here to indulge, then an autumn visit may be rewarded with a 'stag do' as red deer face-off in battle. Or watch out for mountain hares in their wintry white coat – found nowhere else in the UK outside of the Scottish mountains. Elsewhere meadows, rock edges and rivers attract butterflies and birds including rare species like the 'mountain blackbird', the ring ouzel, arriving each spring from Africa and the charismatic dipper (with its own set of swimming goggles).

Less well-known than other landscapes, the unmistakeable cotton ball-like heads of cotton grass bobbing in the breeze of the high tops belie the importance of the peat bogs below – a habitat whose influence on our ability to tackle climate change cannot be overstated.

If the uplands – crowned by Kinder Scout at 2,087 feet (636 m) – are a little too dizzying, why not try the other extreme by delving into the cave networks of Castleton. Whether on foot or by boat, discovering history or the gems of 'Blue John' will take you deep underground, below famed peaks like Mam Tor and the Great Ridge.

With a long and vibrant history of course comes tradition. Summer sees the annual 'well dressing' amongst countless Peak District villages, where a day is never enough to see all the creativity on display. Step into Eyam and you find yourself in the footsteps of history among this famed 'plague village'. Further afield, marvel at the imposing Derwent Dam, that decades ago rumbled to the sound of the Dambusters' Lancaster bombers practising their daring mission.

If literary indulgence is on your list, then you may be just be as inspired as Charlotte Brontë with the diminutive but perfectly-formed North Lees Hall, while less than half an hour's walk will find you atop the same rocks as Keira Knightley from the big-screen adaptation of Pride and Prejudice.

Should the nineteenth century still be a little too contemporary for you, then the Neolithic henge containing many fallen limestone slabs at Arbor Low will certainly transport you back more than a few generations, with other monuments such as the Nine Ladies Stone Circle also offering a glimpse into the area's far and distant past.

As the spiritual home of the countryside access that we all enjoy today, the Peak District always strives to be as pioneering as its forefathers, so what will you take away from your visit to inspire you?

Getting around

The Peak District National Park enjoys a good public transport network, enabling you to reach many areas and enjoy a full day out exploring the area without using the car. Getting to the Peak District couldn't be easier with regular intercity rail services and express coach services from across the UK to destinations around the Peak District from where onward local bus or rail connections are available.

Onward rail services include the Hope Valley Line between Manchester and Sheffield whose stations at Grindleford, Hathersage, Bamford, Hope and Edale give direct access to the spectacular Peak District scenery as well as the Derwent Line (Derby to Matlock), Manchester to Glossop Line, Manchester to Buxton Line and Manchester to Huddersfield Line.
For information: National Rail Enquiries on **08457 484950 www.nationalrail.co.uk.** PLUSBUS adds great value bus travel to your train ticket.

You can get to most parts of the Peak District by bus. The TransPeak bus service from Derby to Buxton runs through the heart of the Peak District, calling at a number of destinations. More information: **www.derbysbus.info**

The Peak District also offers plenty of opportunities to travel by bicycle, with an expanding traffic-free network of trails including the Tissington and High Peak Trail (Ashbourne and Cromford towards Buxton), Monsal Trail (Bakewell towards Buxton) and Manifold Valley Trail (Waterhouses to Hulme End). For tips, routes and more information on cycling within the National Park, see: **www.peakdistrict.gov.uk/visiting/cycle/cycle-routes**

Protecting the countryside

The Peak District National Park Authority wants everyone to enjoy their visit and to help keep the area a special place. You can do this by following the Countryside Code:

RESPECT EVERYONE
- Be considerate to those living in, working in and enjoying the countryside.
- Leave gates and property as you find them.
- Do not block access to gateways or driveways when parking.
- Be nice, say hello, share the space.
- Follow local signs and keep to marked paths unless wider access is available.

PROTECT THE NATURAL ENVIRONMENT
- Take your litter home – leave no trace of your visit.
- Only have BBQs in designated areas and do not light fires.
- Always keep your dogs under control and in sight.
- Dog poo – bag it and bin it in any public waste bin.
- Care for nature – do not cause damage or disturbance.

ENJOY THE OUTDOORS
- Check your route and local conditions.
- Plan your adventure – know what to expect and what you can do.
- Enjoy your visit, have fun, make a memory.

It's pretty easy to act responsibly when out walking. Simply take care not to disturb wild animals and sensitive habitats. Don't take things away like stones or wild flowers, and don't leave anything behind that you shouldn't.

An early start for Walkers on the Great Ridge at Mam Tor

Walking tips & guidance

Safety

Walking will be safe and enjoyable provided a few simple rules are followed:

- Make sure you are fit enough to complete the walk.

- Always try to let others know where you intend to go.

- Take care around cliff edges and keep an eye on the tide.

- Wear sensible clothes and suitable footwear.

- Take ample water and food.

- Take a map or guide.

- Always allow plenty of time for the walk and be aware of when it will get dark.

- Walk at a steady pace. A zigzag route is usually a more comfortable way of negotiating a slope. Avoid going directly downhill as it's easier to lose control and may also cause erosion to the hillside.

- When walking on country roads, walk on the right-hand side facing the oncoming traffic, unless approaching a blind bend when you should cross over to the left so as to be seen from both directions.

- Try not to dislodge stones on high edges or slopes.

- If the weather changes unexpectedly and visibility becomes poor, don't panic, but try to remember the last certain feature you passed and work out your route from that point on the map. Be sure of your route before continuing.

Unfortunately, accidents can happen even on easy walks. If you're with someone who has an accident or can't continue, you should:

- Make sure the injured person is sheltered from further injury, although you should never move anyone with a head, neck or back injury.

- If you have a phone with a signal, call for help.

- If you can't get a signal and have to leave the injured person to go for help, try to leave a note saying what has happened and what first aid you have tried. Make sure you know the exact location so you can give accurate directions to the emergency services. When you reach a telephone call 999 and explain what has happened.

If you call for emergency assistance but are then able to get to a safe area and continue your journey please inform the emergency services again to avoid unnecessary call-outs.

Equipment

The equipment you will need depends on several factors, such as the type of activity planned, the time of year, and the weather likely to be encountered.

Clothing should be adequate for the day. In summer, remember sun screen, especially for your head and neck. Wear light woollen socks and lightweight boots or strong shoes. Even on hot days take an extra layer and waterproofs in your rucksack, just in case. Winter wear is a much more serious affair. Remember that once the body starts to lose heat, it becomes much less efficient. Jeans are particularly unsuitable for winter walking.

When considering waterproof clothing, it pays to buy the best you can afford. Make sure that the jacket is loose-fitting, windproof and has a generous hood. Waterproof overtrousers will not only offer protection against the rain, but they are also windproof. Clothing described as 'showerproof' will not keep you dry in heavy rain, and those made from rubberized or plastic materials can be heavy to carry and will trap moisture on the inside. Your rucksack should have wide, padded carrying straps for comfort.

It is important to wear boots that fit well or shoes with a good moulded sole – blisters can ruin any walk! Woollen socks are much more comfortable than any other fibre. Your clothes should be comfortable and not likely to catch on twigs and bushes.

It is important to carry a compass and a map or guide. A small first aid kit is also useful for treating cuts and other small injuries.

Finally, take a bottle of water and enough food to keep you going.

Public rights of way

Right of way means that anyone may walk freely on a defined footpath or ride a horse or bicycle along a public bridleway. In 1949, the National Parks and Access to the Countryside Act tidied up the law covering rights of way. Following public consultation, maps were drawn up by the Countryside Authorities of England and Wales to show all rights of way. Copies of these maps are available for public inspection and are invaluable when trying to resolve doubts over little-used footpaths. Once on the map, the right of way is irrefutable.

Any obstructions to a right of way should be reported to the local Highways Authority.

In England and Wales rights of way fall into three main categories:

- Public footpaths – for walkers only.

- Bridleways – for passage on foot, horseback or bicycle.

- Byways – for all the above and for motorized vehicles.

Free access to footpaths and bridleways does mean that certain guidelines should be followed as a courtesy to those who live and work in the area. For example, you should only sit down to picnic where it does not interfere with other walkers or the landowner. All gates must be kept closed to prevent stock from straying and dogs must be kept under close control – usually this is interpreted as meaning that they should be kept on a lead. Motorised vehicles must not be driven along a public footpath or bridleway without the landowner's consent.

A farmer may put a docile mature beef bull with a herd of cows or heifers, in a field crossed by a public footpath. Beef bulls such as Herefords (usually brown / red in colour) are unlikely to be upset by passers-by but dairy bulls, like the black-and-white Friesian, can be dangerous by nature. It is, therefore, illegal for a farmer to let a dairy bull roam loose in a field open to public access.

The Countryside and Rights of Way Act 2000 allows access on foot to areas of legally defined 'open country' – mountain, moor, downland, heath and registered common land. It does not allow freedom to walk everywhere. It also increases protection for Sites of Special Scientific Interest, improves wildlife enforcement legislation and allows for better management of Areas of Outstanding Natural Beauty.

How to use this book

Each of the walks in this guide are set out in a similar way. They are all introduced with a simple locator map followed by a brief description of the area, its geography and history, and some notes on things you will encounter on your walk.

Near the start of each section there is a panel of information outlining the distance of the walk, the time it is expected to take and briefly describing the path conditions or the terrain you will encounter. A suggested starting point, along with grid reference is shown, as is the nearest postcode – although in rural locations postcodes can cover a large area and are therefore only a rough guide for sat nav users. It is always sensible to take a reference map with you, and the relevant OS Explorer map is also listed.

The major part of each section is taken up with a plan for each walk and detailed point by point, description of our recommended route, along with navigational tips and points of interest.

Here is a description of the main symbols on the route maps:

Motorway	🚆 Railway station	30m Contour height (m)
Trunk/primary road	🚌 Bus station/stop	Walk route
Secondary road	🚗 Car park	Optional route
Tertiary road	🏰 Castle	❶ Route instruction
Residential/ unclassified road	† Church	Open land
Service road	🗼 Lighthouse	Parks/sports grounds
Track	★ Interesting feature	Urban area
Pedestrian/ bridleway/cycleway	*i* Tourist information	Woodland
Footway/path	🍵 Cafe	Nature reserve
Railway	🍺 Pub	Wetland
Rivers/coast	👫 Toilets	Lakes

WALK 1
Combs

The route climbs from the small village of Combs and offers views of Kinder Scout in the distance.

The pleasant village of Combs fits snugly in a wide hollow beneath Combs Moss – a little known outlier of the Dark Peak. The walk starts and finishes at the Beehive Inn, a focal point of the village.

At the start of the walk the much of the view to the left is dominated by Combs Moss a privately owned grouse moor. The crags of Castle Naze stand out in the distance – this is a favourite training ground for local rock climbers. Behind the rocks and out of sight, a solid earthen bank marks the limits of an Iron Age fort. Parts of the moor have access for 'Right to Roam'.

Approximately halfway round the walk it passes White Hall Outdoor Pursuits Centre run by Derbyshire County Council. This was the first centre of its kind in the UK when it opened in 1951 and it still offers outdoor education activities to local school children and training courses for adults, today.

The small section of road immediately after White Hall follows the old Roman route between Arnemetia (Buxton) and Mancunium (Manchester).

If you are walking on a clear day, the higher ground as you start the return towards Combs allows great views along the valley and to the hills – including Kinder Scout – in the distance.

Distance: 4 miles (6.4km)
Time: 2 hours
Terrain: Moderate; muddy sections, some stiles.
Start/Finish: Roadside, near centre of village (SK042786)
Nearest Postcode: SK23 9UX
Map: OS Explorer OL 24 The Peak District – White Peak Area

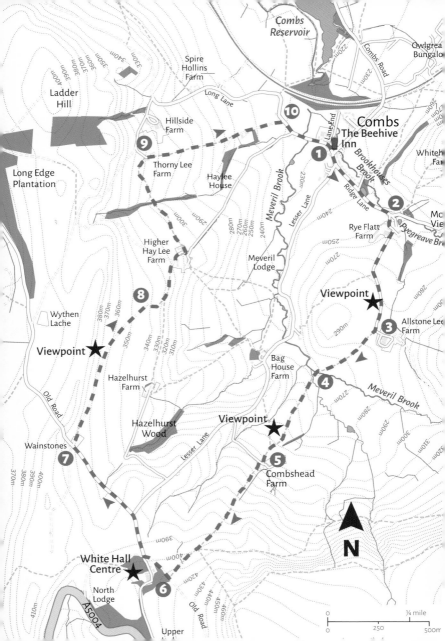

1 Follow the Dove Holes road away from the front of the Beehive Inn for about ¼ mile (400 m).

2 Where the road bears left, turn right along a lane through Rye Flatt farmyard.

3 A few yards beyond a modern bungalow where the lane bears left to Allstone Lee Farm, continue ahead through a gate and along a field path signposted to White Hall.

4 Cross two adjacent footbridges, one stone and the other wood. Climb a series of fields using stiles and gateways.

5 Turn sharp right through Combshead farmyard. Go through a gateway and turn left uphill, for about ½ mile (800 m), beside a wire fence Combs above a shallow gully. Keep to the pathless route by using stiles in field boundaries.

6 Go through a gate and turn right for about ½ mile (800 m) on to a moorland road, then right again beyond the White Hall Centre. After a further 250 m, keep left at a road junction. This section of the road is the part that follows the old Roman route.

7 Turn right opposite the modernised farmhouse of Wainstones. Go past a ruined barn and out along the rough field track beneath a stony ridge for about ½ mile (800 m).

8 After crossing three rough fields, bear right downhill to a walled lane. Follow it left to Haylee Farm. Go right, through the farmyard following the track, at the end of the a stone barn turn immediately left (the footpath goes between the stone barn and a steel framed farm building – as shown.

Cross a small field with a Shepherds Hut on your right to the wooden gate. Cross the next small field to a wall corner, through the next wooden gate follow the path with wall on your right to a stone step over stile. Cross the stile and proceed through a rough field crossing a small stream and keeping the line of trees to your right. At the end of the tree line close to Thorny Lee go through a metal gate then two wooden gates.

9 At Thorny Lee turn right at the end of the stone farm building follow the track downhill until it narrows into a path between two walls. At the end of this go through the metal gate and continue to follow the path downhill keeping the wall on your left (Combs reservoir is visible in the distance). At the next squeeze stile continue on the path downhill, at this point the field boundary changes from a wall to a hedge continue to keep this on your left. At the next squeeze stile with a metal gate you will join a rough track continue on this until the next metal gate. Continue straight on, on the track keeping the farm buildings to your right.

10 At the end of the track turn right and follow the road back to the village.

Castle Naze crags, site of an Iron Age promentory fort, on Combs Moss

WALK 2
Shatton Moor

Tranquil walk which offers some lovely views of Overdale Nature Reserve where meadow pipit, skylark, whinchat, wheatear and curlew may be seen.

Quiet lanes climb the windswept heights to moors which offer unrivalled views across the southern boundary of the Dark Peak. This walk covers a part of the Peak which is often neglected by walkers and is mostly on wide tracks. An added attraction is the opportunity to watch gliders from nearby Hucklow Edge.

This route takes you along the ancient Townfield Lane out of Shatton, part of a saltway which ran up Hurst Clough beyond Bamford. It is also thought to have been on the Roman road from the fort of Navio at Brough over the Long Causeway to Sheffield.

Parking is sparse in Shatton village, so take care not to impede other road users. It might be easier to arrive by train – Bamford Station is only ½ mile from the start of the walk.

1 Walk past the houses and Noe Lane and then turn right onto Townfield lane at the end of the village. Go forwards over a ford and along a tree-lined sunken lane for about ½ mile (800 m), climbing out into open fi elds.

2 Turn right through a gate at the lane end and follow a field track (and a line of electricty poles) to the right of the boundary hedge.

Distance: 4½ miles (7.2 km)
Time: 2¼ hours
Terrain: Moderate;
one 775ft (236m) climb
Start/Finish: Shatton (SK201825)
Public Transport: S33 0BG
Map: OS Explorer OL 1 The Peak
District – Dark Peak Area

3 Beyond the farm buildings go through the gate, follow the path to the left keeping to the right of some trees and the boundary wall.

As you approach point 4 there is a fantastic view over the Edale Valley to Mam Tor ridge.

4 Go through a metal gate and turn left (onto Brough Lane). Follow this rough track along the broad grassy ridge for about 1½ miles (2.4 km).

After about mile you can see a raised earthwork on your right – Grey Ditch. A little further along there is a path which goes off to the right. It leads to Rebellion Knoll from where you get a sectacular view of Bradwell to the west.

5 Go through the metal gate across Brough Lane. Keep left along the sandy track and head towards the open moor.

As the road starts to bear to the north there is a viewpoint over Bretton Clough – Home of the Britons.

6 Walk on, continuing ahead at the junction in the tracks.

At this point a view over Overdale Nature Reserve opens up. It is an upland pasture with sedges, mosses, ferns and lichens, with bracken on the steep valley sides. Meadow pipit, skylark, whinchat, wheatear and curlew have all been recorded in the reserve.

7 Follow the direction of the bridleway signpost to Shatton. Turn left at Wolf's Pit and join a walled lane. Follow this round the shoulder of Shatton Edge, past the TV mast for 1 mile (1.6 km).

8 Bear left downhill on the tarmac road back to Shatton.

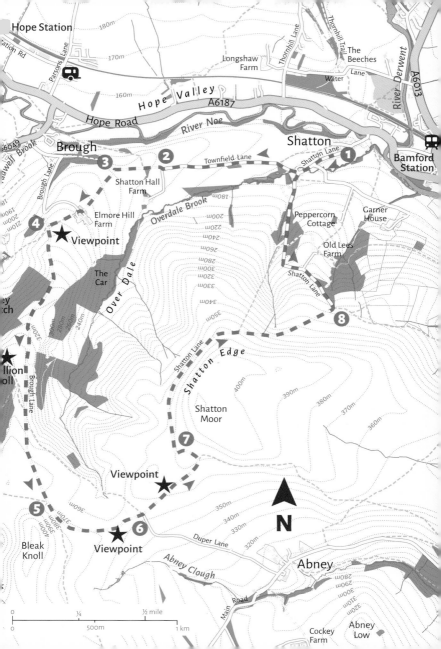

Horse riders on Shatton Lane
on Shatton Edge

WALK 3
Carl Walk and Higger Tor

Easy walk with some boggy sections, with a relatively gentle climb up to Higger Tor where there are lovely views over the Derwent Valley and heather clad moors.

There are many enigmas in the Peak District: stone circles, cairns and burial mounds were left by a community which had no means of conveying their purpose to us. Possibly of slightly later antiquity, Carl Wark hill fort hints of the need for tribes of the time to protect themselves from attack. We cannot tell whether this fort is Iron Age or even post Roman, but what is certain is that it was built in such a way that even the siege of time has had little effect.

1 From the Longshaw Estate car park, walk through the narrow belt of beech woods to the estate lodge. Cross the B6521 to enter a stretch of mixed woodland flanking the A6187 below the Fox House Inn.

2 Turn left and join the A6187 at Burbage Bridge. Take great care crossing the bridge on this busy road and follow the road as far as Toad's Mouth rock.

When viewed from below, the projecting snout and carved eye of Toad's Mouth are what give the rock its name. However many recent visitors have said the resemblance is more like a moray eel.

3 Look out for a stone stile on the right set back from the road about 45 m past the Toad's Mouth rock. Cross it and

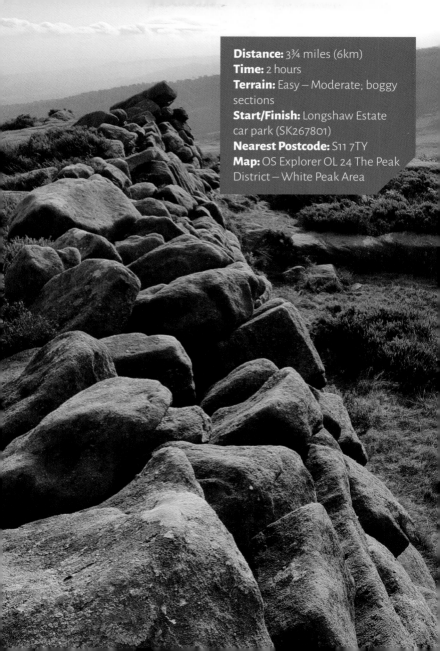

Distance: 3¾ miles (6km)
Time: 2 hours
Terrain: Easy – Moderate; boggy sections
Start/Finish: Longshaw Estate car park (SK267801)
Nearest Postcode: S11 7TY
Map: OS Explorer OL 24 The Peak District – White Peak Area

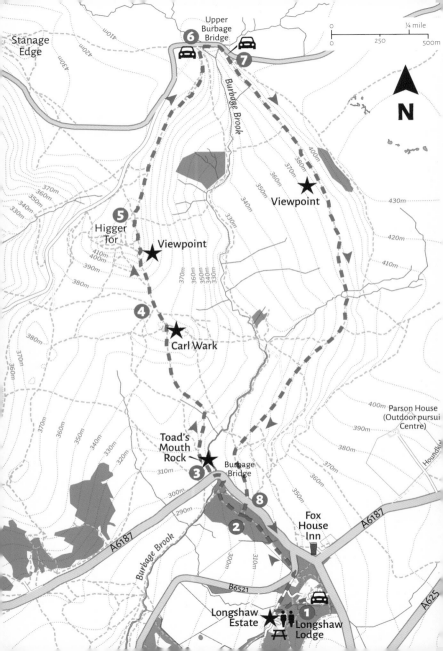

Stanage
Edge

Upper
Burbage
Bridge

6

7

Burbage Brook

Viewpoint

5

Higger
Tor

Viewpoint

4

Carl Wark

Toad's
Mouth
Rock

3

Burbage Bridge

8

Parson House
(Outdoor pursui
Centre)

Houndk

Fox
House
Inn

2

Longshaw
Estate

1

Longshaw
Lodge

A6187

A6187

A625

B6521

Burbage Brook

N

¼ mile

0   250   500

follow an initial rocky path upwards, then through heather and bracken, keeping a boggy area to your right. Above the boggy area, aim for the prominent knoll of Carl Wark.

Carl Wark hill fort. The massive stone walls of the outer perimeter of this defensive point have stood the test of time. Traces of hut foundations and water troughs can still be seen. Notice also how the walls overshadow the two entrance points.

4 Cross the low col beyond the fort and climb the wide path towards the rocks of Higger Tor for ¼ mile (400 m).

As you head towards the Tor stop and look back in the direction from where you have come – the view of Carl Wark on its natural eminence with the Derwent Valley and heather clad moors stretching into the distance is wonderful.

5 Clamber across the summit rocks and follow the escarpment to the right. Follow the moorland path parallel to Fiddler's Elbow road.

6 Cross both the streams beneath the bridges and join the main track descending to your right.

7 Follow the track past a series of abandoned gritstone quarries as far as the main road.

8 Cross the road and go through a kissing gate. Pick up the path and follow back through the trees for about ½ mile (800 m) to the car park.

WALK 4
Birchen Edge

This four mile walk takes you past Nelson's Monument nearby to which there are three boulders known as the Victory, Defiance and Soverin, all of which took part in the Battle of Trafalgar.

Two monoliths erected in memory of Nelson and Wellington make excellent route markers for this walk. The first of these that you encounter is Nelson's Monument. The monument itself is actually a 3 metre tall gritstone column with a ball on the top, and it was erected in 1810. As mentioned above, the monument is located very close to three boulders each shaped like the bow of a man-o-war and named after ships from Trafalgar. The second monument is to Wellington and is in the shape of a stone cross. Wellington's cross was erected in 1866 and from its location there are stunning views over Chatsworth House.

The rest of the route crosses stark gritstone edges on the skyline above Bar Brook, and the whole walk offers magnificent views of the surrounding moors and parkland.

A novel little detour would be to the Eagle Stone. It is slightly off-route but can be reached by a narrow sidepath (near point 6 on the route map). At one time, every young man from Baslow had to climb it before he could get married.

❶ Park near the Robin Hood Inn above the A619 Chesterfield road. Walk past the adjoining cottage and go through the gate on the left. Follow the rocky, woodland path uphill for about ½ mile (800 m), aiming for the crest of Birchen Edge.

Distance: 4 miles (6.4 km)
Time: 2 hours
Terrain: Moderate, with some rocky paths and stiles
Start/Finish: Near the Robin Hood Inn above the A619 Chesterfield road (SK281722)
Nearest Postcode: DE45 1PU
Map: OS Explorer OL 24 The Peak District – White Peak Area

2 Take care on reaching the lower part of the crag and follow the path through a rocky gap, Turn left along the summit rocks.

To the southwest Chatsworth and its parkland fills the valley. Take in the extensive heather-clad landscape to your left.

3 At the triangulation pillar, turn left downhill through a narrow gap in the crag. Turn right along a narrow moorland path, crossing some stone slabbed sections and gently decending for ¾ mile (1.2 km)

4 Go through a gate and turn left on to the road. Follow it with extreme care across the busy A621 Sheffield road. Walk uphill, opposite for about 140 m.

5 Go left through a gate on to a turf covered moorland track. Stay on the track for about 1 mile (1.6 km) at which point you will pass the Wellington monument on the left and a path goes off to the Eagle Stone on the right.

6 Continue on by following the moorland track downhill as far as the moorland boundary.

7 After passing the old quarry on the right, turn hard left and follow the wall and fence into oak woodland. Drop downhill along a faint and windy path through trees for ½ mile (800 m), to a gate and a narrow path around a house.

8 A horse trough to the left of Cupola Cottage marks the way. Walk steadily uphill through the scattered birch wood for ½ mile (800 m).

9 Cross the bracken covered field.

10 After about ¾ mile (1.2 km), climb the stone stile and turn left along the main road back to the Robin Hood Inn.

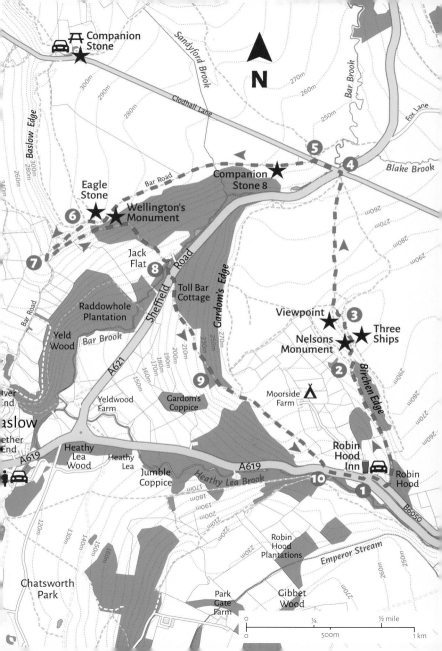

WALK 5
Longnor

This 4 mile (6.4km) walk gives you lovely views over the River Dove which has cut a steep-sided valley through the limestone.

From the village of Longnor, this walk visits two major Peakland valleys. At first, the underlying strata is shale and the River Manifold flows in a broad fertile trough, while across Sheen Moor, the River Dove has carved a steep sided valley through its limestone bedrock.

Longnor village is above the Manifold valley. The walk starts from the market place in the village. The grassy shoulder beyond Longnor marks the boundary between gritstone and shales of the west and the Dovedale limestone of the east. Longnor is a pleasant village boasting a couple of pubs, a café and a selection of small shops.

Looking down into the Dove valley from the viewpoint between Top and Hope Cottage farms, you should see several small hummocks which represent the site of a Norman motte-and-bailey castle.

Just beyond halfway, the walk comes upon the village of Crowdicote. It is named after the Saxon Cruda who built the the first farm on this spot. The Pack Horse Inn is a welcome sight on a hot day.

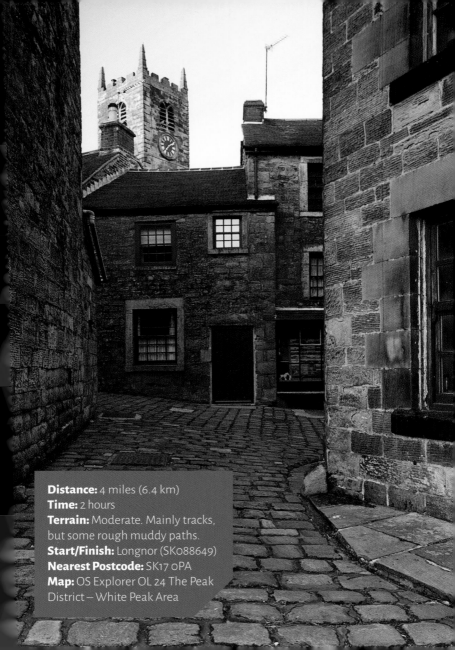

Distance: 4 miles (6.4 km)
Time: 2 hours
Terrain: Moderate. Mainly tracks,
but some rough muddy paths.
Start/Finish: Longnor (SK088649)
Nearest Postcode: SK17 0PA
Map: OS Explorer OL 24 The Peak
District – White Peak Area

1 Follow the road east from Longnor Market Square for about 140 m. Turn right along the signposted lane to Folds Farm. Go left through the farmyard. Climb over a stone stile and turn half right to follow a field path towards the River Manifold.

2 Go through a narrow stile, continuing towards the River Manifold and after about 50 m turn left along a narrow footpath and walk through a series of fields to a gravel surfaced farm track.

3 Turn left along this farm track. Keep left through the farmyard and then right on a concrete track. Through the gate it becomes a rough track. Follow the track uphill for about 1000 m, as far as the road.

4 Turn right along the road for about 460 m, going past Top Farm. Climb the stone stile on the left and turn left, going across three fields. Turn right down the track towards, but not into, Under Whittle Farm.

5 Climb the stile at the top of the farm garden. Follow a waymarked path. Turn right onto a private lane. After about 200 m pick up the waymarked path on the left. Pass a pair of barns and, following waymarks and stiles, cross a series of fields to the River Dove.

6 Cross the river by the footbridge. Follow the track beyond it as far as the lane and turn left into Crowdicote. Go right on the main road, then turn left by Dovemount Cottage along a side lane. After about 100 m turn left to Meadow Farm.

7 Leave the side road beyond the farm. Follow the signpost along a lane to open fields for about ½ mile (800 m).

8 Go over a stile and then left along the wide grassy river access track. Cross the footbridge, then climb a low rise to reach a shallow side valley.

9 Turn left at a stone barn and climb along a gravel lane to Longnor.

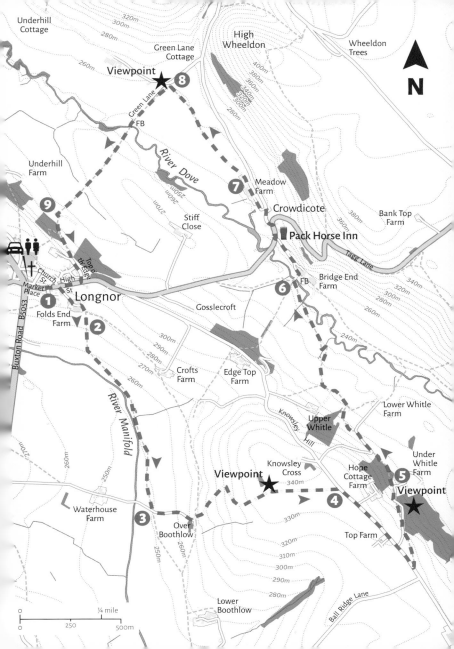

Underhill
Cottage

High
Wheeldon

Wheeldon
Trees

Green Lane
Cottage

Viewpoint ★ **8**

N

Green Lane

FB

River Dove

Underhill
Farm

9

Meadow
Farm

7

Crowdicote

Bank Top
Farm

Stiff
Close

Pack Horse Inn

Tagg Lane

Top o'
th' Edge

Church
St

High
St

Market
Place

1

Longnor

Folds End
Farm

2

FB

6

Bridge End
Farm

Gosslecroft

Buxton Road B5053

River Manifold

Crofts
Farm

Edge Top
Farm

Knowsley
Hill

Upper
Whittle

Lower Whittle
Farm

Waterhouse
Farm

3

Over
Boothlow

Knowsley
Cross

Viewpoint ★

4

Hope
Cottage
Farm

Under
Whittle
Farm

5

Viewpoint ★

Top Farm

Lower
Boothlow

Ball Ridge Lane

¼ mile

250   500m

Chrome Hill and Parkhouse
from the Dove valley

WALK 6
Elton & Robin Hood's Stride

Starting in the village of Elton, once a centre of lead mining, the route takes you past Robin Hood's Stride, where there are the remains of a stone circle, and on to a hermit's cave beneath Cratcliffe Rocks.

This route runs through a historic landscape dominated by lead mine remains and ancient monuments. Lead seams are found running through the limestone and were first mined by the Romans. What is now a rural landscape in some areas was once a hive of industry. At the centre of this walk is the gritstone escarpment of Robins hood stride which is a prominent landscape feature and is popular with climbers.

Elton is a village which once made its living from lead mining. In fact, there was a mine next to the church – you can see where it was from the rough ground next to the church yard. The font inside the church has an unusual history. When the church was rebuilt in Victorian times, the original font found its way to Youlgreave and Elton had to make do with a copy.

Robin Hood's Stride is a gritsone rock tor perched on a ridge at the highest point in the area. It gets its name due to a legend saying that Robin Hood once stood with a foot at each end – despite this being a distance of 15 m! Around 200 m to the east of the tor there is a hermit's cave beneath Cratcliffe Rocks. It is not known who the hermit was but there is a record in the archives of nearby Haddon Hall showing a payment to 'Ye harmytt' for the supply of ten rabbits in 1549.

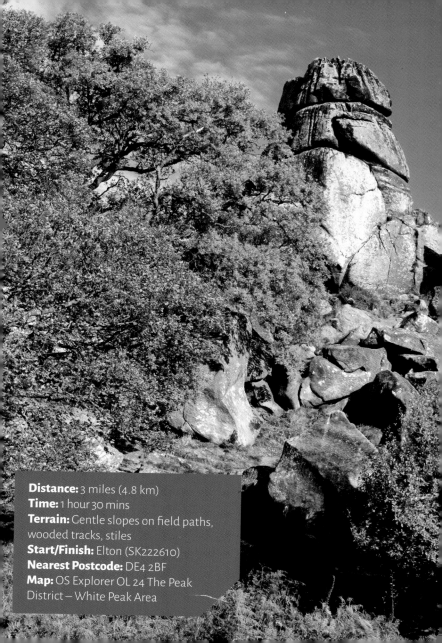

Distance: 3 miles (4.8 km)
Time: 1 hour 30 mins
Terrain: Gentle slopes on field paths,
wooded tracks, stiles
Start/Finish: Elton (SK222610)
Nearest Postcode: DE4 2BF
Map: OS Explorer OL 24 The Peak
District – White Peak Area

1 Turn right by the church down Well Street and walk for 100 m. Fork left track between houses after 50 m. Leave the track and bear left through a gate. Follow the right fork of the field path across the valley for ¾ mile (1.2 km).

2 Cross the minor road, go through a stone squeezer stile opposite and follow a field path for ¼ mile (400 m).

3 Cross the access lane and keep to the left of a prominent knoll. Skirt Tomlinson Wood by following its boundary wall to the left and then a line of telegraph poles for about ½ mile (800 m).

4 Bear left at a rough track and walk for ¼ mile (400 m). Half way down the hill go over a stile to your right and onto the limestone way into mixed woodland.

5 Follow the woodland path as far as the road.

6 Turn right, uphill along the road and then left on a signposted field path. Aim towards the prominent rocks of Robin Hood's Stride about ½ mile (800 m) in the distance.

7 Immediately left of Robin Hood's Stride, follow a side path through bracken and pine wood to the foot of prominent Cratcliffe Rocks to see the Hermits cave. Retrace your steps to Robin Hood's Stride. Turn left to follow the limestone way down the track.

8 Just before the main road head right up the narrower side road for a distance of ¼ mile (400 m).

9 Turn right at a signpost and cross the sparsely wooded slope. Just past the sports field bear slight left across the next field then through the final field and back to the church.

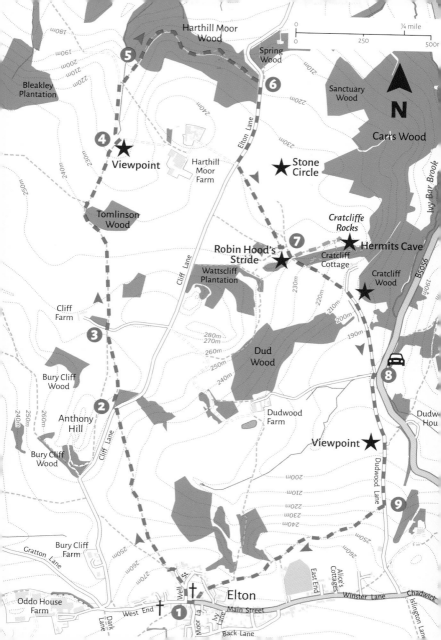

Harthill Moor
Wood

Spring
Wood

5

6

Sanctuary
Wood

Bleakley
Plantation

N

Carrs Wood

4

★
Viewpoint

Harthill
Moor
Farm

★ **Stone
Circle**

*Cratcliffe
Rocks*

Tomlinson
Wood

7

★ **Hermits Cave**

**Robin Hood's
Stride**

Cratcliff
Cottage

Cratcliff
Wood

★

Wattscliff
Plantation

★

Cliff
Farm

3

Dud
Wood

Bury Cliff
Wood

2

8

Dudwo
Hou

Anthony
Hill

Dudwood
Farm

Bury Cliff
Wood

Viewpoint ★

Bury Cliff
Farm

9

Gratton Lane

Oddo House
Farm

Alice's
Cottages

Elton

1

Winster Lane

West End

Main Street

Chadwick

Islington

Back Lane

WALK 7
Three Shires Head

A pleasant walk from a historical village to a collection of pretty pools popular with families and picnickers.

The three shires walk starting from Flash the highest village in England at 1518 feet takes you down a minor road with great views towards Three Shires Head valley. Off the road after passing Wicken Walls Farm a sandy track will take you all the way to Three Shires Head. The return route after climbing a stony track and then another minor road will take you over an old stone clapper bridge and then ascends a rough heather moorland path to Wolf Edge with spectacular views, then public footpaths back to Flash village.

As the name suggests, Three Shires Head lies at the junction of three counties; Derbyshire, Cheshire and Staffordshire. It was once an important crossing point over the River Dane for trains of packhorses. And a place where the horses could be rested and watered. It also had a reputation for lawlessness, with thieves able to evade capture by simply stepping over a county boundary. Today it's a popular spot for families to enjoy picnics and let their children play safely in the shallow pools.

Distance: 4 miles (6.4 km)
Time: 2½ hours
Terrain: Roads and well marked paths, some slopes
Start/Finish: Flash village (SK025672). Park on road side.
Nearest Postcode: SK17 0SW
Map: OS Explorer OL 24 The Peak District – White Peak Area

1 Walk out of Flash village along the minor road to the right of the New Inn. Follow it for ½mile (800 m).

2 Go past the entrance to Far Brook Farm and take the bridle path on the right heading through a gate with a blue arrow. Go down to the stream and bear left once over the stream and along the bridleway. The land owner here allows trial bike riders to practice their skills in this area.

3 Take the footpath towards Wicken Walls Farm buildings a Peak and Northern sign marks the way. Turn right at the farm to reach the lane 160 m.

4 Turn left along the lane which is tarmac at first but later becomes a sandy almost level track for a mile (1.6 km) into the Dane Valley.

5 At Three Shires Head you might want to stop and check out the pools. Once you are ready to continue turn right through the gate and climb the stony track for 180 m.

6 Turn right over a singled arch bridge follow the track to the road then continue along it for another mile (1.6 km).

7 Bear left at the road junction and take the stone clapper bridge to the right to go uphill for about ½mile (800 m) to the heather moor on Wolf Edge crossing the wall at the stiles.

8 Bear diagonally right across the rocky crest of the moor for ½mile (800 m) to join a walled track down to the path junction.

9 Turn right and follow the public footpath back to the road and Flash village.

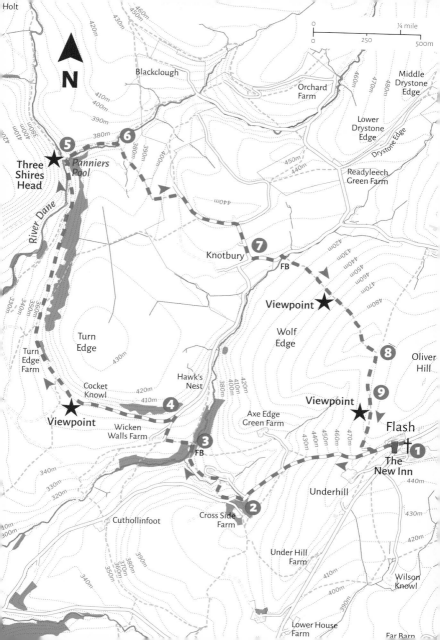

Holt

Blackclough

Orchard Farm

Middle Drystone Edge

Lower Drystone Edge

Drystone Edge

Readyleech Green Farm

5

6

Panniers Pool

Three Shires Head

River Dane

7

Knotbury

FB

Viewpoint ★

Wolf Edge

8

Oliver Hill

Turn Edge

Turn Edge Farm

Hawk's Nest

Cocket Knowl

4

Viewpoint ★

Wicken Walls Farm

3

FB

Axe Edge Green Farm

Viewpoint ★

9

Flash

1

The New Inn

2

Cross Side Farm

Cuthollinfoot

Underhill

Under Hill Farm

Wilson Knowl

Lower House Farm

Far Barn

N

¼ mile

0   250   500m

WALK 8

Pike Low

A taste of the moors with great views of Derwent Edge, the reservoirs and Derwent and Howden Dams. A visit to an ancient burial mound.

This 9km walk includes one long climb out of the valley and paths that can be rough and wet at times. The reward is some great views and the chance to see birds of prey and possibly mountain hares. The Peak District is the only place in England where mountain hares live. In winter the brown summer coats turn almost pure white – so a winter's day with no snow is a good time to look out for them.

Pike Low is a Scheduled Ancient Monument dating from the Bronze Age.

Derwent and Howden Dams were built in the early years of the 20th century to supply water to the cities of the Derby, Leicester, Nottingham and Sheffield. If you are lucky enough to visit after a prolonged wet spell, the sight of the reservoirs overflowing between the towers of the dams makes a spectacular photo. Close to Howden Dam the route passes a small turbine house where electricity is generated from the flow of water from Howden to Derwent.

Ladybower Reservoir was constructed during the Second World War and famously necessitated the demolition and flooding of Derwent Village.

Distance: 5.3 miles (8.5 km)
Time: 3 hours
Terrain: Mainly roads and marked paths, but steep rocky slope and muddy in places
Start/Finish: Fairholmes Car Park (SK172893)
Nearest Postcode: S33 0AQ
Map: OS Explorer OL 1 The Peak District – Dark Peak Area

★ Howden Dam

East Cable Tip Plantation

Beavers Croft

West Cable Tip Plantation

Island Plantation

Chapel Plantation

Bank Clough

Birchinlee West Plantation

Birchinlee

Calfhey Wood

Birchinlee East Plantation

Abbey Tip Plantation

New Close Wood

Cogman Clough

11

10

Jackson Wood

Shireowlers Wood

Shireowlers North Plantation

9

8

Ouzelden Clough

Wrenhey Coppice

Upper Derwent Valley

Shireowlers South Plantation

Walker's Clough

Gores Farm

Gores Plantation

Derwent Reservoir

Hancock Wood

Hancock Plantation

Hollin Clough

7

Near Deep Clough

Far Deep Clough

Millbrook Plantation

6

Ashton Clough

Derwent Dam

★

12

Hollinclough Plantation

Pike Low

★ 400m

5

Memorial to Tip the Sheepdog

Nabs Wood

Derwent Cottage

Lockerbrook Farm

Lockerbrook Coppice

2

Mill Brook

Dovestone Clo

3

Lanehead Cottage

Warren Plantation

4

Wellhead Barn

Ashe Farm

1

Fairholmes

Upper Derwent Visitor Centre

Old House

Derwent Lane

Shooting Lodge

Wellhead

Hagg Side

Haggtor Coppice

Ladybower Reservoir

3

Rough Wood

A57

Ridges Coppice

N

¼ mile

0   250   500m

1 Standing with your back to the Visitor Centre, turn left past the refreshment kiosk and follow the path, towards the dam. On reaching the road turn right and cross the bridge.

2 Stay on the road as it curves away from the dam and climbs steadily. Ignore a tarmac drive that comes in from the left and stay on the road. Ladybower reservoir appears below you to the right and you follow the road for about a mile.

3 Pass the Shooting Lodge and St Henry's (previously a school house) and after 300 m take the signed footpath on the left, over a stile and past a National Trust sign. At the barn keep left up the sunken path. After the second gate, ignore the grassy track to the right. Keep left by the wall.

4 Pass to the right of the house and then keep left, avoiding the path down to your right. Keep climbing. Go through a gate, then follow the track to the right to the National Trust sign for Pike Low. Continue up hill on the obvious stony track.

5 At the highest point of the track you are close to Pike Low burial mound or 'bowl barrow'. As you are on 'Open Access Land' you can divert off the track to visit it, 220 m to the left of the track. A small mound on the highest point of Pike Low, the barrow offers fantastic 360 degree views. Return to the track and carry on towards a conifer plantation.

6 100 m before the conifer plantation the path bears left at a footpath sign. Follow this path, cross a ruined wall and pass another footpath sign. 200 m on from here, is another signpost. Follow the path signed 'Abbey and Howden Dam', keeping the wall on your left. Continue up the gradual slope and go through the pedestrian gate at the top –

7 This is the highest point of the walk.

Descend gradually, following the path north, up the valley. You now see Derwent Reservoir coming in to view. Arrive at a cross roads of paths at the head of Walkers Clough, marked by a cairn (pile of stones).

8 Ignoring the paths descending to your left, continue straight on. At first it is slightly up hill, but after 150 m our path descends to the left past the ruins of Bamford House.

9 The path now meets a ruined wall – continue on, keeping the wall on your left. Gradually descend Abbey Bank with the Howden reservoir and Dam coming into view.

10 At a derelict wall, the path descends steeply past a signpost to Abbey Grange. Follow it to the right, towards Howden Dam. Through the gate at the edge of the forest, continue through the trees to the main reservoir track.

11 Turn left. The next 2 km is easy walking along the side of Derwent Reservoir.

12 Just before Derwent Dam is reached, turn right through a pedestrian gate. At the east tower follow the path or the steps down to the road. Turn right on the road for the short walk back to Fairholmes.

Looking out over the Derwent Reservoir from Derwent Edge

Water flows over Derwent Dam from the Derwent Reservoir

WALK 9
The Thornhill Trot

Great views of Win Hill and Bamford Edge.
A close up of Ladybower Dam and a lovely walk
through a Derbyshire Wildlife Trust Reserve.

This attractive walk includes Ladybower Dam and the famous 'plugholes'. A great sight after wet spells when the reservoir is overflowing.

The walk also climbs the lower slopes of Win Hill. This area, known as Thornhill Carrs, has not been farmed intensively for decades. It is being 're-wilded' by Derbyshire Wildlife Trust and the varied vegetation of grass, scrub and indigenous trees ensures a wide diversity of wildlife.

Passing through the quiet old village of Thornhill the route returns along a disused railway line. The line was built in the 1900's to carry stone for the construction of Derwent and Howden dams.

Disused railways are a great place to find a wide range of plant and tree species, which in turn attract a variety of insects, birds and animals. Now a bridleway, the line was purchased by the Peak District National Park Authority in 1994 and is known as the Thornhill Trail or 'The Rout'.

Distance: 4 miles (6.4 km)
Time: 2 hours
Terrain: Mainly roads and grassy paths, gentle slopes
Start/Finish: Heatherdene Car Park (SK202859)
Nearest Postcode: S33 0BY
Map: OS Explorer OL 1 The Peak District – Dark Peak Area

1 Leave Heatherdene car park by the path that goes past the P+D machine and toilets and follow it for 300 m to Ladybower Dam.

2 Cross the road, but not the dam. Before the pedestrian entrance to the dam take the path diagonally left down the dam embankment. Continue down through regenerating woodland and as the slope levels off bear left on a track by a wooden fence.

3 On reaching the road turn right over the bridge, then turn left along the road for 30 m, until a gate is reached on the right. Go through this and start the climb. Go through a gate, cross the old railway and continue diagonally left uphill for 800 m through the nature reserve. As you approach the top boundary of the reserve you reach a cross-roads of paths. This is the highest part of the walk.

4 Turn left and start the steady descent. Follow the hedge and fence until you arrive at the first houses of Thornhill. Ignoring paths to left and right continue to the road junction. Turn left and walk past an old chapel on the right and a house with a rare Victorian post box built into the wall. After another 80 m turn right by an old red phone box, (now de-commissioned and housing a defibrillator). After 40 m, just beyond Barleyland cottage on the left, turn left through the gate and down a narrow path.

5 The path terminates at the old railway where you turn left. Keep to the railway, passing through cuttings and over embankments. After about 1km pass a small car park and cross the road to continue on the trail. There are great views of Bamford Edge to the right. Cross the path you followed earlier, and follow the trail until you reach the reservoir service road below the western end of the Ladybower Dam.

6 Turn left up the hill to the dam. Cross over the dam. Cross the road and return to Heatherdene.

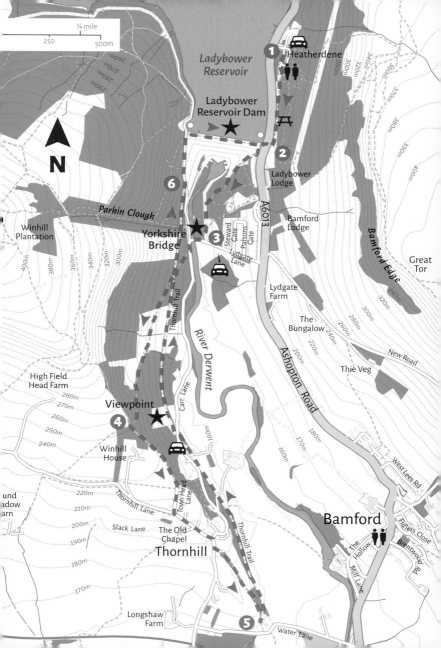

¼ mile

250

500m

1 Heatherdene

Ladybower
Reservoir

Ladybower
Reservoir Dam

★

2

Ladybower
Lodge

A6013

Bamford
Lodge

Bamford Edge

Great
Tor

N

6

Parkin Clough

Winhill
Plantation

Yorkshire
Bridge ★

3

Steward Gate

Parsons Gate

Lydgate
Lane

Lydgate
Farm

The
Bungalow

Thie Veg

New Road

River Derwent

Thornhill Trail

Carr Lane

High Field
Head Farm

Viewpoint

4 ★

Winhill
House

Ashopton Road

Bamford

West Lees Rd

Thornhill Lane

Town Head Lane

Slack Lane

The Old
Chapel

Thornhill

Thornhill Trail

The Hollow

Mill Lane

Fidlers Close

Brentwood Rd

und
adow
arn

Longshaw
Farm

5

Water Lane

View from behind a "plughole" at Ladybower Reservoir Dam, looking towards Bamford Edge

WALK 10
Dovedale

A riverside and hillside walk with the extra fun of some 100 year old stepping stones.

Follow the scenic Dove valley to the historic Coldwall Bridge and the beautiful village of Thorpe returning via the world-famous Stepping Stones. This route can be muddy when wet and after heavy rain the Stepping Stones and paths to the car park may be impassable due to flooding.

The village of Thorpe is a popular stopping point for tourists during the busy season. Its main attraction is the tiny little church, St Leonard's – the current building of which dates back to Norman times. It is said that in medieval times, parishioners of St Leonards kept their arrows at home and used the sandstone porch of the church to sharpen them, leaving the grooves in the church wall that can still be seen today.

Thorpe Cloud, the hill that is skirted during the final third of the walk, gets its name not from any romantic idea of it reaching for the clouds, but from the combination of the Viking word *Thorp* meaning village and Old English *Clud* meaning hill.

The Stepping Stones were first laid circa 1890 as Dovedale became more popular with Victorian tourists. In those days it was even possible to hire donkey rides up Lin Dale.

Distance: 2.9 miles (4.6 km)
Time: 1½ hours
Terrain: Moderate. Can get muddy when wet, stiles and stepping stones
Start/Finish: Dovedale car park (SK146508)
Nearest Postcode: DE6 2AY
Map: OS Explorer OL 24 The Peak District – White Peak Area

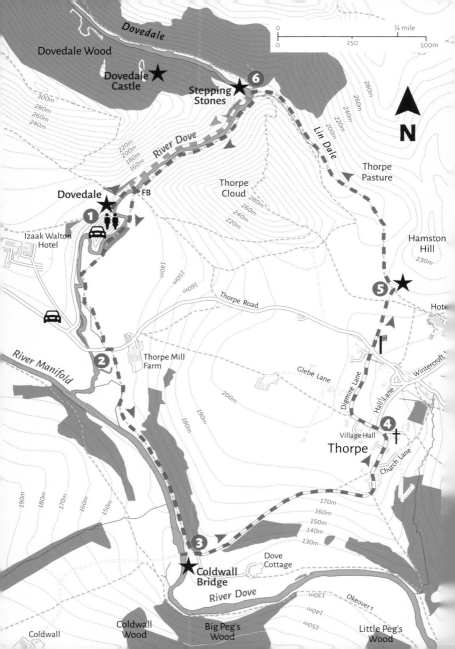

Dovedale

Dovedale Wood

Dovedale Castle ★

Stepping Stones ★ ⑥

River Dove

300m
280m
260m
240m

280m
260m
240m

220m
200m
180m
160m

Lin Dale

200m
220m

240m

Thorpe Pasture

Dovedale ★ ①

FB

Izaak Walton Hotel

Thorpe Cloud

280m
260m
240m
220m

Hamston Hill
230m

⑤ ★

Hotel

140m

150m

160m

Thorpe Road

River Manifold

②

Thorpe Mill Farm

200m

Glebe Lane

Digmire Lane

Hall Lane

Wintercroft

Village Hall

④ ✝

Church Lane

Thorpe

190m
180m
170m
160m
150m

180m

190m

170m
160m
150m
140m
130m

③ ★ Coldwall Bridge

Dove Cottage

River Dove

130m

Okeover 1

140m

150m

Coldwall

Coldwall Wood

Big Peg's Wood

Little Peg's Wood

N

1 Walk out of the car park past the toilets, following the path towards Dovedale. Cross the footbridge on your right then immediately right over the first stile. Follow the footpath through several gates and stiles to the road.

2 At the road turn left, look for the finger post and wicket gate in the wall on opposite side. Follow the footpath over a stile, a wicket a gate, stay on lower path following the River Dove to Coldwall Bridge.

3 On the bridge turn left, go through the metal gate, along the old coach road continuing uphill to a metal vehicle gate and along the road into Thorpe Village. Pass the church on your right.

4 Follow the road from the church past the village hall to a T junction with a bus shelter. Walk up the track left of the bus shelter to a wicket gate and out onto Access land. Follow the track straight ahead.

5 The track arrives at an old quarry. From here turn left, then follow Lin Dale down to the Stepping Stones, keeping the fence line and Thorpe Cloud on your left. (Ascending Thorpe Cloud, will add distance/climb to your walk)

6 Either cross the Stepping Stones following the road opposite to the car park or, for confident walkers, stay on the left bank, following the rocky path across steep screes to the footbridge which you cross to access the car park.

WALK 11
Pack Horses and Iron Horses

A super little walk or cycle through the Manifold Valley, accessible to all

In the heart of the Southwest peak lies the beautiful Manifold valley, which less than one hundred years ago was a busy place with a steam railway serving the villages and creamery. The hillsides were scarred by mining for copper and lead. Tourists used the narrow gauge railway to marvel at the dramatic limestone scenery and the River Manifold that mysteriously disappears underground in summer. The railway's main function however, was to transport milk from dairies such as Ecton to the standard gauge railway at Waterhouses.

Today the railway has gone but has left tracks for walking and cycling and places to stop and enjoy the tranquillity of a slow flowing river and wildlife, which has reclaimed the valley. They are ideal for families and those needing easy access. There is also a café next to the river for relaxing and recharging.

The bridge at Wetton Mill and the track past Dale Farm were built by the Duke of Devonshire in 1807 to transport copper ore from the mine at nearby Ecton. Teams of up to 18 horses carried the heavy copper ore across the bridge.

For an added diversion, there are some caves in the field above Wetton Mill to explore. Follow the public footpath between the house and holiday cottages, turning left after the gate and climbing above the mill. The large caves were formed by melt water flowing through them after the ice age. Take care if you go, as there are some steep drops.

Distance: 2.8 miles (4.5 km)
Time: 1½ hours
Terrain: Fairly level, mainly tracks and minor roads. Tunnel – still used by vehicles (take care when walking through)
Start/Finish: Car park near Wetton Mill (SK094560)
Nearest Postcode: DE6 2AG
Map: OS Explorer OL 24 The Peak District – White Peak Area

Along the river you may see dippers and grey wagtails. Both species feed on minibeasts found in clean unpolluted rivers.

① From the car park, walk over the old packhorse bridge towards Wetton Mill. Once over the bridge turn left towards Dale Farm and follow the track past the camping field to the edge of the farmyard.

② Do not go into the farmyard but turn left just before (signed Hulme End 2½) and pass through the wooden gate to continue along the track. Sheep are often in these fields, so please keep dogs on leads. The track is level at first then slowly climbs. Soon the river appears below the track and there are some good spots for a picnic or quiet reflection. Go through two metal gates before reaching a third at checkpoint 3.

③ Pass through the metal gate, taking care as you join the minor road. The route is now shared with vehicles although it is not usually busy with traffic. Turn left (signed Wetton Mill, Butterton, Wetton) and cross over the river.

④ Once over the river take the minor road on the right (signed Manifold Valley, Wetton Mill, Wetton) bending round to go through Swainsley Tunnel (a single track but well lit) and continue along the minor road back to the parking places at Wetton Mill.

⑤ Arrive back at the car park where you started. Below the bridge next to the car park is a lovely spot for picnics and watching the river and maybe a duck or dipper if you're lucky. Or why not cross the bridge to the café for a well-earned ice cream?

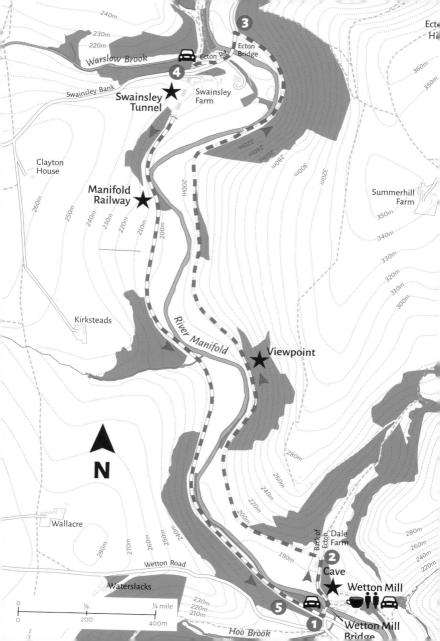

240m
230m
220m
Warslow Brook
Ecton Rd
Ecton Bridge
3
4
Swainsley Bank
Swainsley Tunnel
Swainsley Farm
Clayton House
360m
350m
Manifold Railway
Summerhill Farm
350m
340m
260m
250m
240m
230m
220m
210m
200m
220m
240m
260m
280m
300m
320m
Kirksteads
River Manifold
200m
Viewpoint
330m
320m
310m
300m
280m
N
280m
260m
240m
220m
200m
190m
Back of Ecton
Dale Farm
2
Cave
280m
260m
240m
220m
Wallacre
Wetton Road
260m
250m
240m
Waterslacks
230m
220m
210m
5
1
Wetton Mill
Wetton Mill Bridge
Hoo Brook

0   ⅛   ¼ mile
0   200   400m

WALK 12
Millers Dale

A strenuous walk which takes you up (and down) both flanks of the River Wye valley

This is a circular walk with splendid views of the Wye Valley and White Peak landscape. The prominent hamlet of Priestcliffe, presents some fine panoramic views and examples of medieval ridge & furrow landscape features, making a striking contrast with the gentle sheltered feel of the dale bottom. Here, the former textile mill at Litton today it is a beautiful tranquil spot to look out for river life including water voles & kingfishers if you are lucky. However, during the industrial revolution the Mill had a sinister reputation for the ill-treatment of its workers, many of whom were children.

There is a steep ascent past the quarry and a steep descent down to the Monsal Trail, both of which are difficult after rain.

1 From Millers Dale Station walk east (crossing the viaduct) for 550 m until you reach a sign post where a footpath crosses the Monsal Trail, and there is a pub sign "The Anglers Rest". Take the footpath right signed "Miller's Dale Quarry" up to a gate.

2 Climb steep path diagonally to your left through meadow to another gate. Follow footpath through gate continuing upwards. The path then swings right to metal field gate. Continue uphill alongside fence (ignore DWT Nature Walk signpost) to reach drystone wall at top.

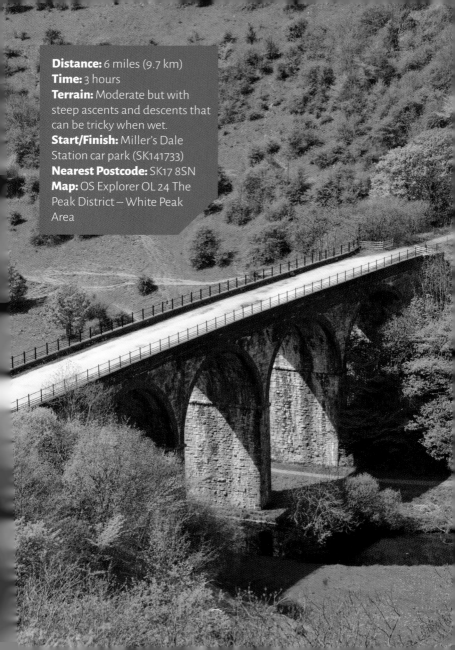

Distance: 6 miles (9.7 km)
Time: 3 hours
Terrain: Moderate but with steep ascents and descents that can be tricky when wet.
Start/Finish: Miller's Dale Station car park (SK141733)
Nearest Postcode: SK17 8SN
Map: OS Explorer OL 24 The Peak District – White Peak Area

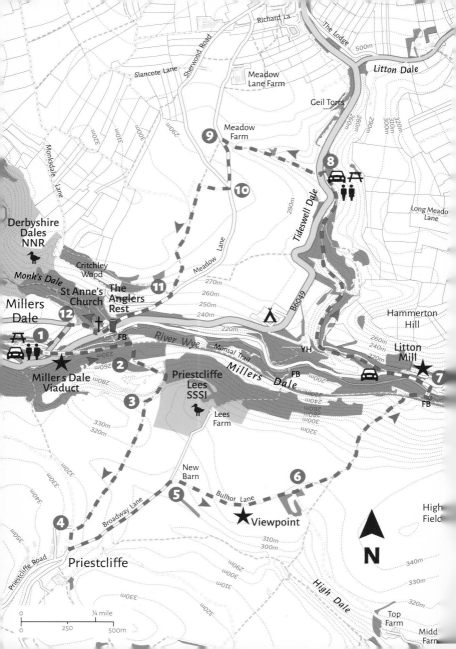

3 At top, cross the stile and walk straight ahead crossing several drystone walls via stiles and gates to reach lane at Lydgate Farm at edge of Priestcliffe Village.

4 Turn left onto lane and past farm buildings, then left onto Broadway Lane, signposted "Brushfield" and "Lees Farm". Follow road straight for 0.5 km (5-10 mins) to reach prominent building of New Barn.

5 Turn right here and follow Bulltor Lane for another 0.5 km (5-10 mins) until another sharp right bend. Go straight on and enter Derbyshire Wildlife Trust Priestcliffe Lees Nature Reserve.

6 Continue ahead passing old mine workings, then cross wooden stile, keep left downhill. After wooden gate descend steep path down to Monsal Trail. Cross over Trail following path down to footbridge. Cross river near Litton Mill.

7 Turn left onto metalled road to reach footpath on right signed "Tideswell Dale". Follow path through Dale to Tideswell Dale Car Park. At this point the path divides at a bridge but joins again later so take either.

8 Continue through car park, cross over road and follow the footpath opposite. The path rises gently up a valley towards Meadow Farm.

9 Follow concessionary footpath left of Meadow Farm behind barn ruin to reach road. Turn left walking about 250 m down road to T-junction with farm track opposite.

10 Follow track (bridleway) for 150 m to reach footpath that crosses track. Turn left down footpath through fields and over stiles for 650 m to reach minor road. NB Bridleway and footpath can be muddy in wet weather.

11 Turn right and follow road (Meadow Lane) to reach main road. Turn right and continue until St Anne's Church. Turn right onto footpath, climb steps and follow path uphill to reach stile by road.

12 Turn left and walk down road to Millers Dale Station.

Litton Mill, site of a notorious former textile mill, now apartments

WALK 13

Bygone Blackwell

Journey through the ages, from Romano-British settlements, to the Midland Railway in 19th & 20th Century, and passing a short distance from one of Europe's largest limestone quarries of today.

The walk starts by following the Wye. This is both scenic and excellent for seeing wildlife including dippers and water voles.

At the top of the steep path from the river, look to your right – the hummocky ground is cultivation terraces and building remnants of a Romano-British settlement dating from 400AD.

After about a third of the walk you reach the highest point at Blackwell. As you head away from Blackwell on a bridleway towards Chee Dale, Tunstead Quarry comes into view on the other side of the valley. Established in 1920, it is the largest supplier of lime and lime-based products in the UK, extracting 5-6 million tonnes of limestone per annum for the chemical and other industries, including toothpaste manufacture.

At Blackwell Mill, there were three railway lines forming a triangle – the Buxton branch line, the mainline to Manchester and the connecting line between, which is still used for freight.

Shortly after joining the Monsal Trail you will walk through Rusher Cutting Tunnel – as you approach the tunnel, notice the naturally eroded cliffs on the right/south side vs cliffs on the left side which are manmade, blasted & cut out when the railway was built in the 1860s.

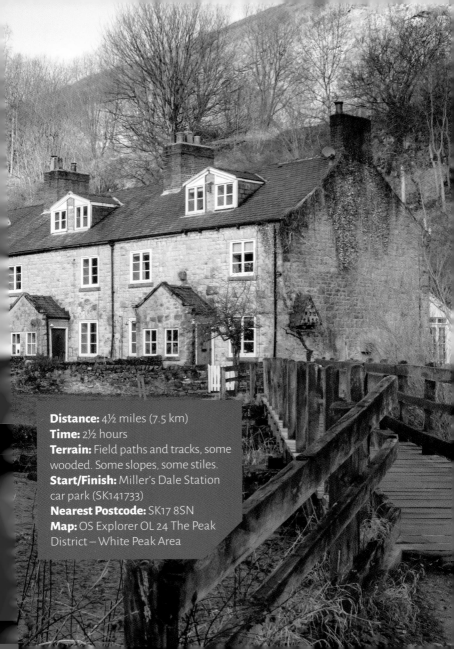

Distance: 4½ miles (7.5 km)
Time: 2½ hours
Terrain: Field paths and tracks, some wooded. Some slopes, some stiles.
Start/Finish: Miller's Dale Station car park (SK141733)
Nearest Postcode: SK17 8SN
Map: OS Explorer OL 24 The Peak District – White Peak Area

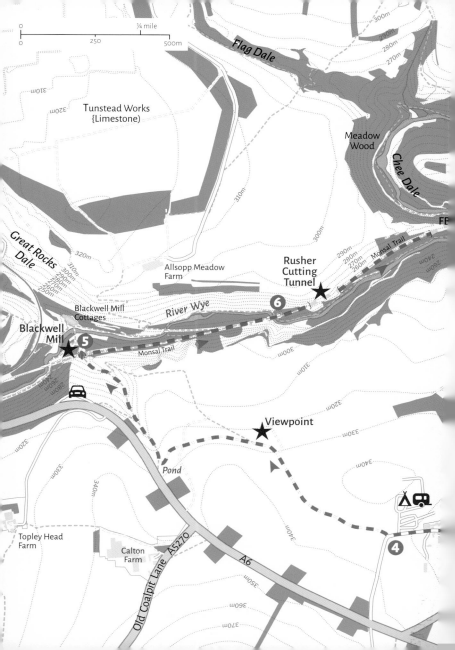

Critchley Wood

Monksdale Lane

260m

Derbyshire Dales
National Nature
Reserve

240m
220m

260m
240m
220m

2

FB

River Wye

290m

280m

Millers
Dale
Station

Monsal Trail

Chee Tor
Tunnel

FB

Wye Valley Footpath

1

★ Millers Dale
Viaduct

★ Viewpoint

260m
250m
240m

280m

290m

300m

Blackwell Dale

B6049

250m

280m

290m

280m

290m

300m

340m
330m
320m

330m
320m

330m
340m

Blackwell
Hall

3 🚐

Blackwell Dale

Long Lane

N

Blackwell

Priestcliffe

Broadway
Lane

Priestcliffe
Ditch

340m
350m

380m
370m
360m

Priestcliffe Road

Hollow O'The Moor

1 With the station buildings on your right, walk to the end of the platforms and down the steps on the left. Before the road, take the stone stile/gap in wall on the right, follow the river for 1 km (15 minutes) to a footbridge.

2 Go over the footbridge, and uphill to the left. At the fingerpost, take the footpath on the right, signed Blackwell, which heads steeply uphill. Follow this path across several fields and onto a track for 1.25 km into the yard of Blackwell Hall Farm.

3 At the end of the farm buildings, veer right to leave the farm road and take the path over a stone stile and through a small wooded area - follow it across 3 fields into the hamlet of Blackwell and turn right at the lane.

4 After the campsite, the lane turns sharply to the left. Follow the track/bridleway signed to Chee Dale 3/4 on the corner for 1 Km. Before reaching the road, go through the gate on the right marked "Nature Reserve" and follow the track downhill.

5 Take the bridge over the old railway and go through the gate on the left which takes you onto a former railway line – now the Monsal Trail. You are at Blackwell Mill - turn left onto the Trail – signposted Bakewell.

6 Follow the trail for 3 Km back to Millers Dale Station car park. You will pass through three tunnels, over a viaduct and look down into Chee Dale. Take a moment to look at the Lime Kilns on your left.

RUSHER CUTTING TUNNEL

WALK 14
Grindsbrook and the Sled Route

An adventurous walk to the edge of Kinder Scout Plateau via the valley of Grindsbrook, with great views across the Edale valley.

There are some steep sections with some rocky scrambles and the path can be very muddy after rain. This outward route follows the stream of Grindsbrook as it winds its way up the valley. You might spot dippers and grey wagtails along the stream, and red grouse and kestrels overhead.

The return route to Edale follows the old 'sled road' which was used by the villagers to bring down peat cut from the moor for their fires. The 'sleds' were homemade sledges constructed by replacing the wheels of haycarts with sledge runners.

Edale is a smashing little village with some interesting buildings. The pretty church of the Holy and Undivided Trinity was built between 1885 and 1886 – it replaced a 17th-century chapel that stood across the road within the old graveyard. The Nags Head pub built in 1577 and was formerly the village blacksmiths. It marks the official start of the Pennine Way.

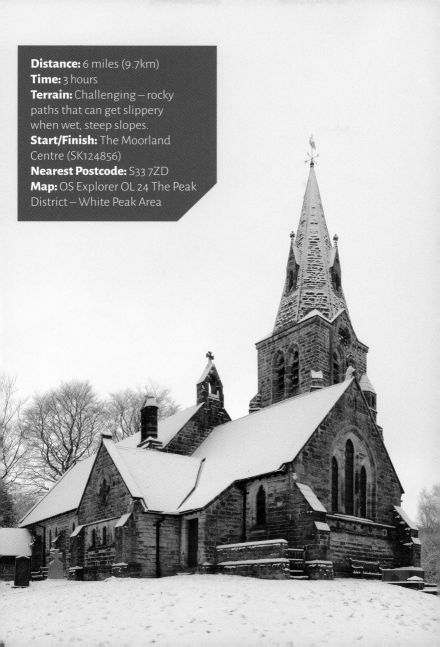

Distance: 6 miles (9.7km)
Time: 3 hours
Terrain: Challenging – rocky paths that can get slippery when wet, steep slopes.
Start/Finish: The Moorland Centre (SK124856)
Nearest Postcode: S33 7ZD
Map: OS Explorer OL 24 The Peak District – White Peak Area

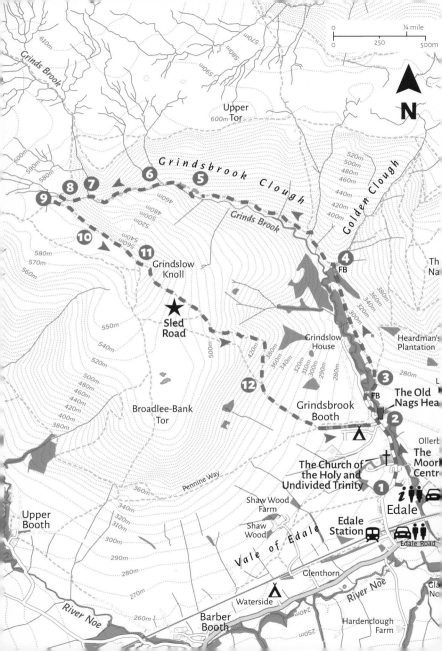

1 Exit the Moorland Centre and turn right on the road, passing the church to reach The Old Nag's Head pub.

2 Continue straight ahead on the road, keeping to the left of the pub. Just before the lane goes through the gate towards "The Gathering", take the footpath down to the right. Cross a narrow bridge and then climb the stone steps.

3 At the top of the steps, follow a stone slab path to the left. This takes you all the way to a gate into a wooded area. Continue through the trees, to another gate.

4 Leave the wood through the gate, then cross a narrow humped bridge. Head left up some stone steps, then follow the path as it bears right and winds its way up the valley, keeping the river down to your left.

5 The path drops down to the river beneath the boulders at Halfway Rocks. This section is rocky and often very wet, so take care – As an alternative, it's possible to follow a path above the rocks, then drop back to the main path.

6 As you leave Halfway Rocks, carry on up the rocky path, and go through a gate in the fence.

7 The rocky path now closely follows the river, crossing it at one point. As you reach a fork in the river, follow the left fork.

8 The climb becomes steeper towards the head of Grindsbrook Clough. Continue up the steep rocky scramble beside the stream (be prepared to get wet!) Eventually, you will reach a huge cairn (pile of rocks) at the top of the valley. You've made it!

9 Once you have finished celebrating, look back down the way you came. Just to your right is a path heading along the edge of the valley to a high point (Grindslow Knoll). Follow this path.

10 Continue along the path, with the edge falling away immediately to your left. Just before reaching the top of Grindslow Knoll, take the left fork in the path, heading just below the summit.

11 Continue to skirt Grindslow Knoll and follow the path as it heads downwards. This descent is steep and rocky at first, but soon becomes easier. Pass through a gate and follow the path downhill to eventually pass through another gate.

12 Follow the path as it sweeps left through fields. At a signpost, turn right on the Pennine Way, and follow the tree-lined path back to the Old Nag's Head. Turn right on the road to return to the Moorland Centre.

WALK 15
Langsett

Linger at Langsett's oasis or loop along the woodland water-front promenade.

Langsett is one of a number of reservoirs built in Victorian times that form Sheffield Lakeland. It lies a little way to the west of the city and about 2km to the south-west of Penistone. Enjoy a walk on wide, well-maintained footpaths through diverse woodland with chance to admire the stunning views across the water to the open heather moorland beyond.

The main walk is fairly level and not too long but it may be too difficult for wheelchair users or those with mobility issues. There is a short walk at this location which is accessible to all.

Optional Short Walk: Start from the rear right-hand corner of the car park and follow the field-edge path until a path is met on the left. Descend along the woodland path until a turning on the right to a clearing with a pond and seating. Return the way you came.

Distance: 2 miles (3.3 km)
Time: Around an hour
Terrain: Fairly level, well marked paths.
Start/Finish: Langsett Barn (SE211004)
Nearest Postcode: S36 4GY
Map: OS Explorer OL 1 The Peak District – Dark Peak Area

Main Walk: **1** Start from the rear right-hand corner of the car park and take the lower path.

2 Go through the gateposts down a steep slope to the reservoir side.

3 Continue along a well-surfaced level woodland path and up a climb to meet a forest track.

4 Turn right and follow the track uphill through the woodland before making a right turn and continuing parallel to, but at some distance from, the main road before meeting the field-edge path back to the car park.

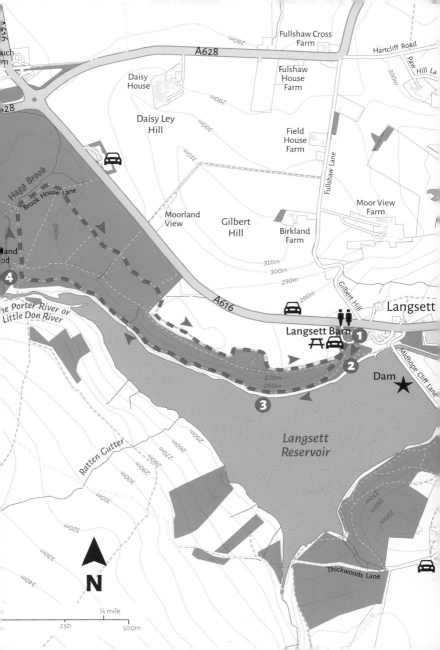

Fullshaw Cross Farm

A628

Hartcliff Road

Paw Hill La

Daisy House

Fulshaw House Farm

280m

Daisy Ley Hill

290m

300m

Field House Farm

Fullshaw Lane

Moor View Farm

Hagg Brook

Brook House Lane

280m

Moorland View

Gilbert Hill

Birkland Farm

310m
300m
290m

Gilbert Hill

Langsett

4

The Porter River or Little Don River

A616

280m

Langsett Barn

1

2

Midhope Cliff Lane

Dam ★

270m
260m

3

Langsett Reservoir

Ratten Gutter

250m

260m

270m

280m

290m
300m
310m
320m

330m

340m

250m

280m
290m

270m

Thickwoods Lane

N

¼ mile

250

500m

Langsett Dam. The valve tower was built to replicate the gatehouse of Lancaster Castle

WALK 16
Longstone Ashford Loop

Take a stroll to explore some 'lost' villages in and around the beautiful Wye Valley.

A gentle walk, showcasing 3 fine examples of Peak District communities of past & present.

Begin in the bustling market-town of Bakewell, one of the largest towns within the National Park. It's ideally situated on the River Wye and showcases a fantastic medieval Grade-I listed 5-arch bridge. Pause in the streets to admire the pretty stone buildings or pop into a café to enjoy one of the infamous Bakewell Puddings.

Great Longstone presents a fine example of a vibrant White Peak village, with a village shop, 2 pubs, and a primary school, set beneath the long gaze of Longstone Edge. The town's station, originally opened in 1863, closed in the 1960s and after the line itself closed in 1968 became an interesting stopping point on the 8.5 mile Monsal Trail.

Meanwhile, Ashford-in-the-Water is a picturesque riverside community, with a jumble of pale limestone cottages demonstrating the 'White Peak' character of the southern half of the Peak District National Park. There are several listed buildings in the village including two Grade II* – Sheepwash Bridge, a packhorse bridge dating back to the 17th century – and Ashford Hall.

Distance: 6 miles (9.7 km)
Time: 3 hours 15 minutes
Terrain: Well marked paths, gentle slopes.
Start/Finish: Tourist Information Centre car park (SK218685)
Nearest Postcode: DE45 1DS
Map: OS Explorer OL 1 The Peak District – Dark Peak Area

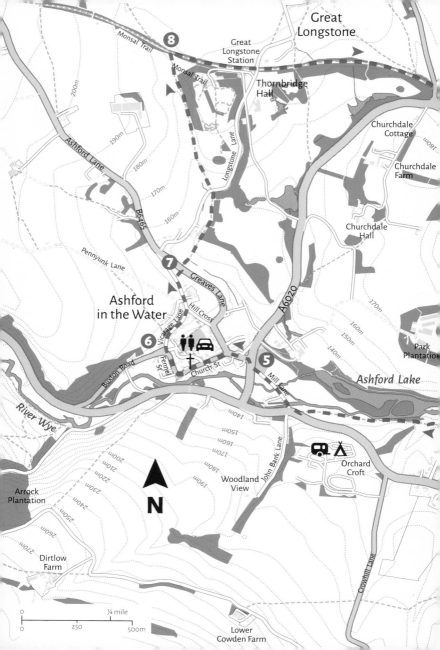

1 Turn right from Visitor Centre, walk along Bridge Street, and cross bridge. Turn left following sign to Scott's Garden. Walk upstream across field through two gates.

2 Head towards finger post and go through wooden gate, to reach Holme Lane. Turn left, walk past Lumford Cottages. Cross over the bridge to join road (A6).

3 Turn right on road, continue past supermarket on right. 200 m later turn right onto footpath, opposite Deepdale Business Park. Go through stone squeeze (gap), walk across field and along path between houses.

4 Cross road and stile, pass through wicket gate and walk across fields above River Wye. Go through gate to join A6. Turn right, then after 50 m, turn right again on old road, cross two bridges and continue to main road near cricket pitch.

5 Cross the road and follow straight ahead into Ashford-in-the-Water. Stay left, passing the shop and church then following Fennel Street round to right. After 100 m reach a grass island, (Toilets are available if you turn right and follow the lane for 50 m).

6 At island, continue straight up Vicarage Lane and pass Highfield Farm on right. After 100 m, pass through stone squeeze gate on right and along path to road (B6465).

7 Cross the road and follow footpath opposite, downhill between walls. Continue in direction of signpost finger (north). Follow path across fields beside the wall. Cross Longstone ('Shady') Lane. Follow the footpath opposite across fields, until reaching the Monsal Trail.

8 At Bakewell Station, turn right, walk through car park, join road (Station Road). Turn right and descend steep hill towards Bakewell town centre. At junction, turn left and cross bridge. After 100 m you will arrive at Visitor Centre.

The remains of Great Longstone Station, on the Monsal Trail

WALK 17
Goyt Valley

Rivers, Ruins and Ridges on a bracing walk with fantastic views.

The Goyt valley and surrounding moorlands give a great introduction the gritstone moors of the Peak District. Rising up from the Cheshire Plain they have a feeling of wildness and are shaped by the elements. The walk starts next to Errwood Reservoir constructed to provide water for nearby Stockport, flooding farmsteads and changing the character of the valley forever. An easy to follow route with a challenging climb, woods, moors and great views.

Near the start of the walk it passes the ruins of Errwood Hall where you are free to explore. Errwood Hall was built in 1840 for the wealthy Grimshawe family. It stood for less than 100 years as it was demolished in 1934 when the reservoirs were being built. The Hall overlooked the hamlet of Goyts Bridge, which is now entirely under water.

There is an optional addition to the summit of Shining Tor, which is well worth doing if you have the energy. At 559 m above sea level, the summit of Shining Tor is the highest point in Cheshire. On a clear day you can see right across to Snowdon in Wales!

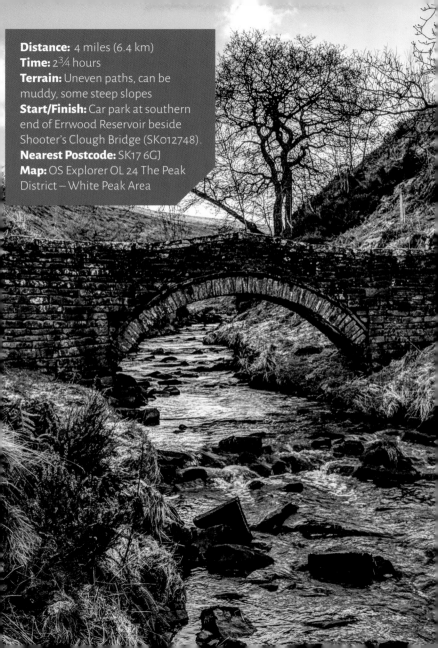

Distance: 4 miles (6.4 km)
Time: 2¾ hours
Terrain: Uneven paths, can be muddy, some steep slopes
Start/Finish: Car park at southern end of Errwood Reservoir beside Shooter's Clough Bridge (SK012748).
Nearest Postcode: SK17 6GJ
Map: OS Explorer OL 24 The Peak District – White Peak Area

1 From the car park, follow the dirt path uphill for about 100 m (past benches for an early picnic with great views over the reservoir). Pass through the gap in the stone wall and continue straight ahead, following the sign to Errwood Hall. After about 300 m there is a set of stone steps and then a track on the right hand side. Detour here to explore the ruins of Errwood Hall (great for hide and seek, adventures, and picnics).

2 Back on the track, continue uphill with the stream on your left. After about 300 m turn left at a crossroads, signed 'Stakeside'.

3 Follow the dirt/stone path for about 350 m, with the stream on your left, until the path crosses the stream. There is no bridge but the stream is usually shallow, with lots of stones. Note: This is a good turning-around point for very small children (simply follow your route back to the car park).

4 Continue to follow the path as it zig-zags uphill through the woods, following signs to 'Stakeside' until after 650 m you pass through a wooden gate onto the moorland. Turn right here (signed 'Cat & Fiddle') and follow the dry stone wall uphill. Note: To reduce this route to a shorter 3km walk, turn left here and walk downhill back to the car park (as for point 11).

5 Continue uphill for 1.2 km until the path levels out at the brow.

Optional: From here head up a flagged path to the summit of Shining Tor, the route is signposted. Retrace your route back down.

6 Continue along the path, with the wall on your right, signed to 'Cat & Fiddle'. After about 200 m pass through a wooden kissing gate then continue straight ahead, along the path between a dry stone wall on your left and wire fence on your right.

On a clear day, the views from the summit of Shining Tor are stunning

7 At the end of the path (after 600 m) pause to admire the spectacular views over the Cheshire Plain and (on a clear day) the Welsh hills. Then, turn right past a log barrier and head downhill for 250 m towards the Peak View Café.

8 From the café, follow the footpath along the tarmacked farm driveway, which starts just uphill from the café. Just before the farmyard, go through a metal kissing gate on the right and into the field.

9 Follow the path along the edge of the field, uphill and through a second metal kissing gate, and then through the wooden kissing gate which you've seen already at point 6.

10 Continue to the detour point to Shining Tor, and then follow the path straight ahead, gently downhill for 1.2 km to reach the wooden kissing gate from point 4.

11 Continue straight ahead, following the grassy track downhill towards the reservoir. You will pass through a wooden kissing gate and after about 750 m the path becomes sandy. Continue straight ahead at the crossroads (signed 'Errwood Car Park') and follow the path through the woodland to reach the car park.

WALK 18
Crowden

Explore this beautiful valley on the route of the Pennine Way.

A short distance from the reservoirs of the Longdendale Valley and the busy Woodhead pass running between Manchester and Sheffield lies the Crowden valley. Whilst on the route of the Pennine way it soon becomes a tranquil place of woodland, moorland and streams. The walk is an out and back route meaning that you can go as far as you feel with places to stop and enjoy the surrounding views or have a picnic next to a stream. This is an easy to follow route with a good surface for all the family to enjoy.

On the walk watch out for evidence of badgers in the area. You probably won't see any of the mammals themselves but Brockholes Wood is a nature reserve and the name Brock is an old name for a badger. You can often see their tracks or holes where they have been.

The two rivers in the Crowden Valley are the Crowden Great Brook and the Crowden Little Brook. After they meet their water continues downsteam into the Torside Reservoir. Water from this reservoir is used to provide drinking water for Manchester.

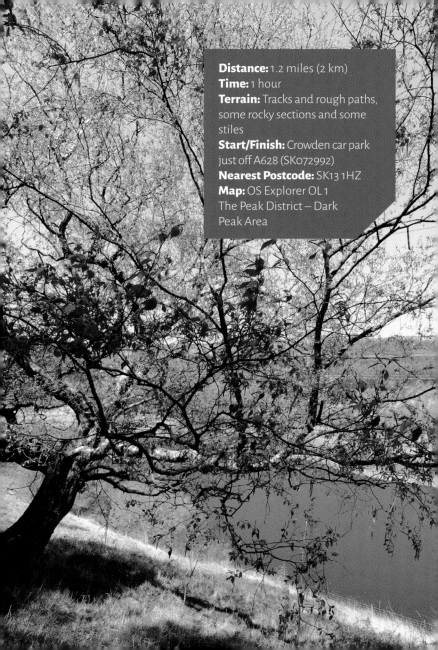

Distance: 1.2 miles (2 km)
Time: 1 hour
Terrain: Tracks and rough paths, some rocky sections and some stiles
Start/Finish: Crowden car park just off A628 (SK072992)
Nearest Postcode: SK13 1HZ
Map: OS Explorer OL 1 The Peak District – Dark Peak Area

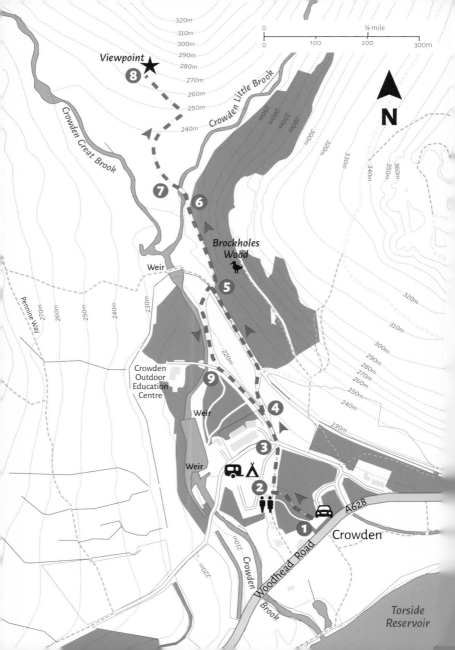

320m
310m
300m
290m
280m
270m
260m
250m
240m

Viewpoint ★

8

Crowden Little Brook

250m
260m
270m
280m
300m
320m
330m
340m
350m
360m

Crowden Great Brook

7

6

Brockholes Wood

Weir

5

320m
310m
300m
290m
280m
270m
260m
250m
240m
230m

Pennine Way

270m
260m
250m
240m
230m
220m

Crowden Outdoor Education Centre

9

Weir

4

3

Weir

2

1

A628

Crowden

Woodhead Road

Crowden Brook

210m
220m

Torside Reservoir

⅛ mile

0   100   200   300m

N

1 Take the tarmac path at the corner of the car park, next to the information board.

2 When you reach the public toilets, turn right on the path and pass the campsite.

3 By the entrance to the campsite, continue straight ahead to cross the lane and go through a gate, following the tarmac track which heads towards Crowden Outdoor Education Centre.

4 At a fork, leave the tarmac track to follow the grassy track heading uphill to reach a stile and a gate. Turn left in front of these, passing through a metal gate. Continue on this narrow path beside a water channel.

5 At the end of the path, go through the gate and turn right on the rocky track, which crosses a stone bridge and bends to the left, passing Brockholes Wood nature reserve. Continue on the track to a gate.

6 Go through the gate and turn immediately left to cross the wooden bridge over the river (Crowden Little Brook) onto a flat, grassy area. This is a lovely spot to picnic, but please remember to take your rubbish home.

7 To reach a fantastic viewpoint, bear right after crossing the bridge and head for the metal gate. Cross the stile next to the gate and follow the track as it zigzags uphill to a flat, rocky spot.

8 Retrace your steps down the hill, across the bridge and through the gate to the right. Continue along the track, following as it curves to the right and heads downhill. Keep on the track to a junction with a tarmac lane.

9 Turn left along the lane, and retrace your steps back to the car park.

WALK 19

Mam Tor via the Great Ridge

Head up to the summit of the Mam Tor or "Shivering Mountain" taking in the iconic Great Ridge along the way.

This route has great views of the Hope and Edale Valleys, but should be avoided in high winds as the ridge is very exposed.

Step back in time as you take in the old coffin route at Hollins Cross. Before Edale got its own church, this old route was used from Edale to the parish church at Castleton. Mourners used to stop for prayers at Hollins Cross before continuing to Castleton.

Mam Tor itself is 517 m above sea level. The summit provides stunning views in all directions on all but the bleakest days. It used to be an Iron Age Settlement and there is evidence of hillfort ramparts circling the summit.

Perhaps one of the most popular parts of the walk takes you over the old broken road. Once it was a well used road allowing vehicle access into the valley, but the unstable geology of grit and shale layers of Mam Tor meant that there were constant landslides. In 1979, the repeated reconstruction and repair of this road was abandoned but the amazing formations created by landslips on the broken road were left as an unusual visitor attraction.

Listen out for skylarks singing along the ridge and enjoy the coconut-scented gorse flowers.

Distance: 6 miles (9.7km)
Time: 3 hours
Terrain: Strenuous walk, with steps and grassy paths – can be muddy in wet with exposed ridge section (should be avoided in high winds)
Start/Finish: Castleton car park (SK149830)
Nearest Postcode: S33 8WN
Map: OS Explorer OL 1 The Peak District – Dark Peak Area

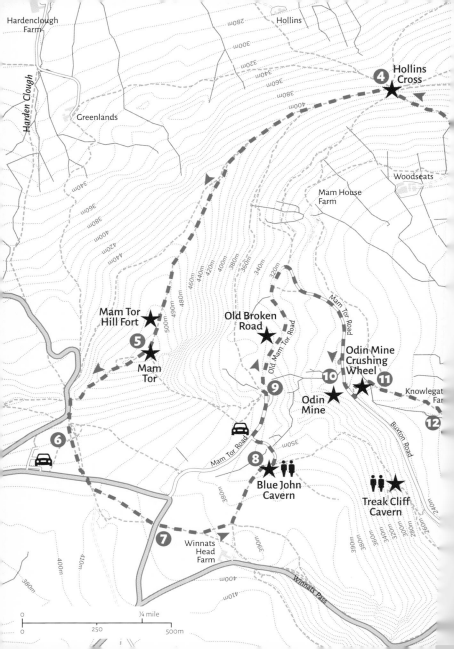

Hardenclough Farm

Harden Clough

Hollins

Greenlands

Hollins Cross

4

Woodseats

Mam House Farm

Mam Tor Hill Fort

Old Broken Road

Odin Mine Crushing Wheel

5

Mam Tor

11

Knowlegat Far

Mam Tor Road

9

10

Odin Mine

12

6

Old Mam Tor Road

Buxton Road

Mam Tor Road

8

Blue John Cavern

Treak Cliff Cavern

7

Winnats Head Farm

Winnats Pass

0
¼ mile
250
500m

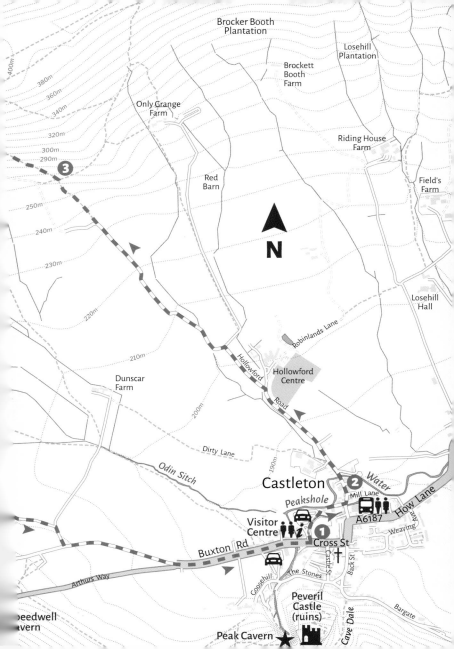

① From the Visitor Centre entrance, cross straight over the road leading into the car park and turn left to follow the stream. At the corner of the car park, join a lane heading to the right with a stream on your left. Turn left when you meet Hollowford Road.

② Follow the road out of the village. At the Hollowford Centre, bear left on the road and continue to follow the road as it turns left at the next junction. Continue on this road until it bears sharply left – at this point go straight ahead through the gate to join a track heading uphill, signposted Public Bridleway to Hollins Cross.

③ Pass through a gate at the top of the track and join a rocky track uphill, which crosses the hillside diagonally to the left and passes through several gates before reaching the summit of the ridge at Hollins Cross. This path can be wet, muddy and slippy in bad weather.

④ At Hollins Cross, turn left to follow the flagged (paved) path along the ridge. Pass through 2 gates and keep left uphill to reach the summit and trig point of Mam Tor. This ridge can be very exposed and windy in bad weather.

⑤ From the summit, descend down the stepped path. As you approach the road, the path bears left downhill to a gate. Pass through this gate and down a few steps to another gate that leads to a field.

⑥ Go straight downhill to gate at bottom of slope. Cross the road to gate on the other side to enter field. Bear left onto a grassy track leading to next gate. Do not follow rough track straight ahead. Instead, cross the road again and go through a gate into another field.

7 Go straight ahead through field to a gate in the stone wall. Head left diagonally across the field on a faint track passing by a white gate structure and downhill with a marshy dip on your left to gate that leads to Blue John Cavern buildings.

8 Pass buildings and take tarmac road to the left and follow it steeply uphill to next road. Turn right and follow the road to the end by a turning circle. Pass through the gate to join the old Broken Road.

9 Cross the stream (which can be tricky) and follow the old broken road downhill. The road is rough and cracked so care is needed. Go through the next gate and follow the road downhill to the right to a metal gate near a pond.

10 Pass through the gate and continue on the road, and after a bus turning circle take a path on the left to the Odin Mine Crushing circle. This is one of the oldest lead mines in Derbyshire and possibly the UK, with the peak of the mining occurring in 17th century. The mine ceased work sometime around 1870.

Follow the path keeping the crushing circle on your right to cross a stream.

11 Carry on downhill, taking care as the path can be wet and slippy, passing through a gate, over a stile and down some steps to Knowlesgate farm.

12 Turn right uphill onto farm track. pass through metal gate and continue on road which eventually bends to the right to join the main road. Turn left to continue down the road to return to the Visitor Centre.

A beautiful misty morning on the Great Ridge

WALK 20
Damflask Loop

Enjoy a circuit of Damflask Reservoir from the pretty village of Low Bradfield. Keep a look out for birds in the woodlands.

In the heart of Sheffield Lakeland and a short distance from the city lies Damflask Reservoir, one of a series of reservoirs built in Victorian times to accommodate the growing demand for water from the nearby city. Today the reservoir is surrounded by woodland, which in spring is full of birdsong. The path around the shores is well surfaced and easy to follow and level making it accessible to all. The breaks in the trees offer great views. There are many good picnic spots along the way making it a great day out for the family.

Damflask reservoir was completed in 1896. It is 27 m deep at the deepest point and it can hold 4,250.9 million litres of water – that is over 42,000 household baths! The reservoir is a great place to spot birds. Some species that you might be able to see are mallard, mute swan, Canada goose, blue tit, great tit, blackbird, kestrel.

❶ From the car park, cross the footbridge towards the cricket ground. Once over the bridge keep heading to the left and go through a gap in the wall ahead to reach a lane.

❷ Public toilets are situated to the left here, but to continue the walk, turn right on the lane. Pass the village post office, where refreshments are available, and continue past the cricket pitch to a road junction by the Smithy Garage.

Distance: 3½ miles (5.5 km)
Time: 2 hours
Terrain: Tarmac lanes, good level tracks — suitable for all
Start/Finish: The Sands car park (SK262920) — also served by 61 bus (from Hillsborough)
Nearest Postcode: S6 6LB
Map: OS Explorer OL 1 The Peak District — Dark Peak Area

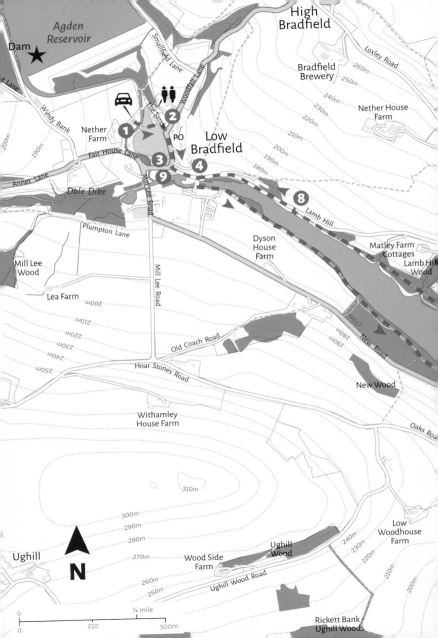

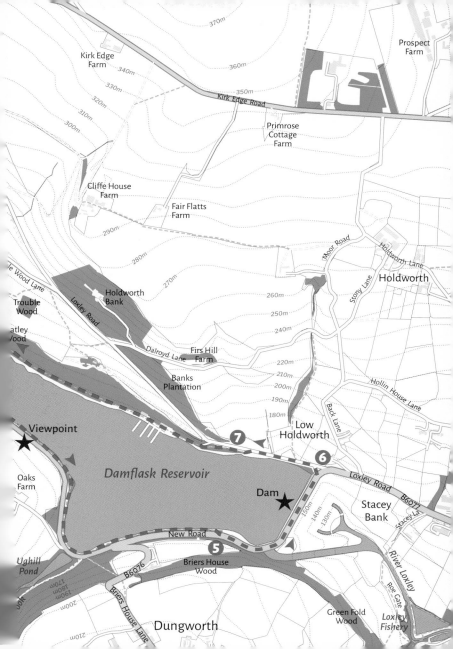

❸ Turn left in front of the Smithy Garage to walk along the quiet lane, Lamb Hill. Continue a short distance to reach a lane on your right.

❹ Turn right on the lane to cross a bridge. Immediately afterwards, turn left on the footpath, which leads along the south side of Damflask Reservoir.

❺ Near the end of the reservoir, the footpath takes you through an opening in the fence and onto a road, turn left at the road and follow it around to the dam wall.

❻ Once across the dam, turn left onto Loxley Road for a short distance, before going through a gap in the wall on your left and onto a footpath.

❼ Follow the footpath along the north side of the reservoir, past the sailing and rowing club. Continue on the path until it eventually meets the Lamb Hill Road.

❽ Turn left on the road and follow it back to the village of Low Bradfield.

❾ Turn right at the Smithy Garage, cross the road, and return over the playing fields to the car park.